Better Homes & Gardens.

CHRISTMAS COOKING
FROM THE HEART.™

Giving is Receiving

Meredith. Consumer Marketing
Des Moines, Iowa

CHRISTMAS COOKING
FROM THE HEART™

MEREDITH CORPORATION CONSUMER MARKETING
Consumer Marketing Product Director: Heather Sorensen
Consumer Marketing Product Manager: Janece Schwartzkopf
Consumer Marketing Billing/Renewal Manager: Tami Perkins
Business Manager: Diane Umland
Senior Production Manager: Al Rodruck

WATERBURY PUBLICATIONS, INC.
Editorial Director: Lisa Kingsley
Creative Director: Ken Carlson
Associate Editor: Tricia Bergman
Associate Design Director: Doug Samuelson
Production Assistant: Mindy Samuelson
Contributing Copy Editor: Peg Smith
Contributing Proofreader: Terri Fredrickson
Contributing Food Stylist: Jennifer Peterson
Contributing Photographer: Doug Samuelson

***BETTER HOMES AND GARDENS*® MAGAZINE**
Editor in Chief: Stephen Orr
Art Director: Jennifer D. Madara
Senior Deputy Editor: Nancy Wall Hopkins
Editorial Assistant: Renee Irey

MEREDITH NATIONAL MEDIA GROUP
President: Tom Harty

MEREDITH CORPORATION
Chairman and Chief Executive Officer: Stephen M. Lacy

In Memoriam: E.T. Meredith III (1933–2003)

Copyright © 2017 by Meredith Corporation.
Des Moines, Iowa.
First Edition. All rights reserved.
Printed in the United States of America.
ISSN: 1083-4451   ISBN: 978-0-696-30247-3

Our seal assures you that every recipe in *Christmas Cooking from the Heart*™ has been tested in the *Better Homes and Gardens*® Test Kitchen. This means that each recipe is practical and reliable and it meets our high standards of taste appeal. We guarantee your satisfaction with this book for as long as you own it.

All of us at Meredith® Consumer Marketing are dedicated to providing you with information and ideas to enhance your home. We welcome your comments and suggestions. Write to us at: Meredith Consumer Marketing, 1716 Locust St., Des Moines, IA 50309-3023. *Christmas Cooking from the Heart*™ is available by mail. To order editions from past years, call 800/627-5490.

Cover: Cranberry Layer Cake with Sparkling Juice (cake recipe, page 82)

APPLE-WALNUT
DOUGHNUTS,
PAGE 54

LAMB MEATBALLS
WITH CRANBERRY
DRIZZLE, PAGE 33

Table of Contents

Giving is Receiving

During the holiday season, there is perhaps no better way to show the important people in your life how cherished they are than to cook or bake something magnificent and share it with them. The gift of time spent in the kitchen and the end result is meaningful and beloved. *Better Homes and Gardens® Christmas Cooking from the Heart™* can help you create a special holiday season for loved ones this year—from Thanksgiving feasts to intimate New Year's Eve gatherings. For a lavish family dinner, choose Beer-Braised Brisket (page 10) or Grilled Turkey Breast with Spiced Almond Butter (page 13). For a celebratory brunch, try Bagel and Lox Skillet Strata (page 45) or Blueberry-Peach Custard Kuchen (page 50). And, of course, the holiday's wouldn't be complete without decadent desserts—indulge in Berry-Walnut Upside-Down Cake (page 80), Bananas Foster Crème Brûlèes (page 86), or Hot Cocoa Souffle with Coffee Ice Cream (page 91).

Happy Cooking—and Happy Holidays!

SUGAR COOKIE
CUTOUTS, PAGE 103

ROASTED CHICKEN
WITH GRAPES, PAGE 13

Celebration Dinner Party

Of all the meals you anticipate throughout the year, this one is the pinnacle of celebratory dining—the holiday feast. Whether it's an intimate gathering for close family or a big bash, these dishes will frame this memorable event.

BEER-BRAISED BRISKET

BEER-BRAISED BRISKET

PREP 30 minutes
COOK 10 minutes
BAKE 3 hours 30 minutes at 325°F

1	3½- to 4-lb. flat cut corned beef brisket or beef brisket, trimmed, leaving ¼-inch layer of fat
1	tsp. sea salt
1	tsp. cracked black pepper
1	Tbsp. vegetable oil
3	Tbsp. coarse ground mustard
2	tsp. dried sage, crushed
3	onions, halved and thinly sliced
3	carrots, coarsely chopped
2	stalks celery, coarsely chopped
4	cloves garlic, peeled and smashed
1	12-oz. bottle brown ale
1	cup water
¼	cup tomato paste
1	recipe Celery-Horseradish Garnish

1. Preheat oven to 325°F. Season beef on both sides with salt and cracked pepper. Heat oil in a 4- to 5-quart Dutch oven. Brown meat well on both sides, cutting in half to fit if necessary. Remove from heat; turn meat fat side up. Spread with mustard and sprinkle with sage. Add onions, carrots, celery, and garlic to pot.

2. In a medium bowl whisk together ale, the water and tomato paste. Pour over meat. Bring to boiling over high heat. Cover and transfer to oven. Bake 3½ to 4 hours or until fork tender.

3. Transfer meat to a cutting board to cool slightly. Meanwhile, prepare sauce by pureeing cooking liquid and vegetables in the Dutch oven with an immersion blender (or cool 15 minutes and transfer to a blender). Season to taste.

4. Thinly slice meat across the grain. Arrange on a platter and top with some of the sauce. Pass remaining sauce. Top with Celery-Horseradish Garnish. Makes 12 servings.

Celery-Horseradish Garnish In a small bowl combine ¾ cup chopped celery leaves, ⅓ cup chopped fresh parsley, 1 tablespoon prepared horseradish, and ½ teaspoon kosher salt.

PER SERVING *412 cal., 32 g fat (12 g sat. fat), 91 mg chol., 498 mg sodium, 7 g carb., 1 g fiber, 3 g sugars, 22 g pro.*

CHIANTI-BRAISED STUFFED MEAT LOAF

PREP 40 minutes
BAKE 55 minutes at 350°F

- 2 eggs, lightly beaten
- ⅔ cup shredded Parmesan cheese
- ½ cup seasoned fine dry bread crumbs
- ½ cup thinly sliced green onions
- ½ cup snipped fresh basil
- ¼ cup tomato paste
- ¼ cup Chianti or other dry red wine
- 2 cloves garlic, minced
- ¼ tsp. salt
- 2 lb. ground beef sirloin
- 1 recipe Cheese Filling
- ½ cup Chianti or other dry red wine
- 2 Tbsp. Chianti or other dry red wine
  Fresh snipped basil and/or Italian parsley

1. Preheat oven to 350°F. In a large bowl combine first nine ingredients (through salt). Add ground beef; mix well. Divide meat mixture in half. Pat each portion into a 9×5-inch rectangle.

2. Place one meat portion in a 9×13-inch baking dish, building up edges to make a 1-inch-deep well in center. Spoon Cheese Filling into well. Top with remaining meat portion; pinch top and bottom edges together to seal. If necessary, gently reshape into a 9×5-inch loaf. Pour the ½ cup wine into dish around loaf.

3. Bake 50 to 60 minutes or until meat is done (160°F). Spoon the 2 tablespoons wine over meat loaf. Garnish with basil and/or parsley. Makes 8 servings.

Cheese Filling In a bowl combine 1 cup (4 oz.) shredded mozzarella cheese; ½ cup chopped, toasted pine nuts (tip, page 14); ½ cup finely chopped oil-packed dried tomatoes; 3 tablespoons snipped fresh basil; 1 tablespoon oil from jar of dried tomatoes; and ½ teaspoon lemon zest.

PER SERVING *428 cal., 26 g fat (8 g sat. fat), 134 mg chol., 506 mg sodium, 11 g carb., 2 g fiber, 2 g sugars, 33 g pro.*

CHIANTI-BRAISED
STUFFED MEAT LOAF

GRILLED TURKEY
BREAST WITH
SPICED ALMOND
BUTTER

GRILLED TURKEY BREAST WITH SPICED ALMOND BUTTER

PREP 30 minutes
FREEZE 10 minutes
GRILL 1 hour 45 minutes
STAND 10 minutes

⅓ cup butter, softened
⅓ cup finely chopped slivered almonds or chopped pine nuts
¼ cup snipped fresh parsley
1 tsp. lemon, orange, or tangerine zest
1 Tbsp. lemon, orange, or tangerine juice
2 large cloves garlic, minced
½ tsp. ground allspice or ground ginger
½ tsp. freshly ground black pepper
1 5- to 6-lb. whole turkey breast with bone (thawed, if frozen)

1. For the Spiced Almond Butter, in a small bowl combine all of the ingredients except the turkey. Cover and chill in freezer 10 minutes or in refrigerator 20 minutes or until easy to handle.
2. Starting at the breast bone, slip your fingers between skin and meat to loosen skin, leaving skin attached at the sides to make a pocket. Spread the slightly chilled butter under skin of turkey.
3. To protect from burning on the grill, cover the outside of a shallow roasting pan with heavy foil. Place the turkey, breast side up, on a rack in the roasting pan. Insert a meat thermometer into the thickest part of breast (not touching bone).
4. Prepare grill for indirect medium heat. Place turkey in roasting pan on grill rack in center of grill. Cover; grill 1¾ to 2 hours or until thermometer registers 170°F.
5. Remove turkey from grill and cover loosely with foil. Let stand 10 minutes before carving. Makes 8 servings.
PER SERVING *485 cal., 26 g fat (9 g sat. fat), 185 mg chol., 168 mg sodium, 2 g carb., 1 g fiber, 0 g sugars, 57 g pro.*

ROASTED CHICKEN WITH GRAPES (PHOTO, PAGE 8)

PREP 20 minutes
COOK 25 minutes
BAKE 1 hour 50 minutes at 350°F

2 whole roasting chickens (3- to 3½-lb. each)
6 thick slices bacon, chopped
1 tsp. paprika
Kosher salt and black pepper
2 lemons, halved
4 cups seedless red and/or green grape bunches
½ cup medium yellow onion, halved and sliced
1 shallot, finely chopped
2 cloves garlic, minced
8 oz. button mushrooms, sliced
1 Tbsp. tomato paste
1 cup dry white wine
¼ cup heavy cream
2 sprigs fresh thyme

1. Preheat oven to 350°F. Remove neck and gizzards from chickens. Rinse chickens and pat dry. Tuck wings under and secure drumsticks.
2. In a large skillet cook bacon until browned and crisp. Remove; drain on paper towels, reserving drippings. Cover and refrigerate bacon. Combine 2 tablespoons drippings (or melted butter) and paprika; brush over chickens. Sprinkle with kosher salt and pepper.
3. Place chickens in 7- to 8-quart oval Dutch oven or roasting pan. Arrange lemons around chicken. Bake, uncovered, 1½ hours.
3. Using turkey baster, remove ⅔ cup pan juices; skim off fat and set aside for sauce. Tuck bunches of grapes around chickens in pan. Return to oven; bake 20 to 30 minutes or until thermometer registers 175°F in the thighs.
4. Meanwhile, for sauce, in skillet cook and stir onion, shallot, and garlic in 2 tablespoons drippings for 4 minutes or until softened. Add mushrooms; cook and stir 5 minutes or until browned. Stir in tomato paste. Add wine and ½ cup reserved pan juices; cook and stir until thickened and bubbly. Stir in cream and herb sprigs. Boil gently, uncovered, 5 minutes or until thickened. Stir in bacon. Pass the sauce. Makes 10 servings.
PER SERVING *581 cal., 42 g fat (12 g sat. fat), 142 mg chol., 186 mg sodium, 13 g carb., 1 g fiber, 10 g sugars, 35 g pro.*

PERFECT TURKEY GRAVY

START TO FINISH 15 minutes

1 to 2 cups reduced-sodium chicken broth
Pan drippings from roasted turkey
2 to 4 Tbsp. melted butter (optional)
¼ cup all-purpose flour
Salt and black pepper

1. Stir 1 cup broth into pan drippings from roasted turkey in roasting pan, stirring to scrape up any crusty brown bits from bottom of pan. Pour drippings into a 2-cup glass measuring cup. Skim and reserve fat from drippings. If necessary, add enough melted butter to reserved fat to equal ¼ cup. Add enough broth to drippings to equal 2 cups.
2. Pour the ¼ cup fat into a medium saucepan (discard any remaining fat). Stir in flour.
3. Add broth mixture all at once to flour mixture in saucepan, stirring until smooth. Cook and stir over medium heat until thickened and bubbly. Cook and stir 1 minute more. Season to taste with salt and pepper. Strain gravy into a serving bowl. Makes 8 servings.
PER SERVING *76 cal., 6 g fat (2 g sat. fat), 7 mg chol., 288 mg sodium, 3 g carb., 0 g fiber, 0 g sugars, 1 g pro.*

Creamy Cracked Pepper and Garlic Gravy Prepare gravy as directed, except before adding flour to the fat in Step 2, add 3 cloves garlic, minced, to the fat; cook and stir over medium heat about 2 minutes or until garlic is fragrant and beginning to brown. Stir in flour. Stir in ¼ cup heavy cream and 2 teaspoons Worcestershire-style marinade for chicken with the broth mixture in Step 3. Continue as directed. After straining gravy, stir in 1 teaspoon cracked black pepper. If desired, stir in 1 tablespoon snipped fresh parsley. Makes 2¼ cups (8 servings).

LEMONY SPINACH PESTO

START TO FINISH 15 minutes

1 lemon
1½ cups packed fresh spinach
⅓ cup slivered almonds, toasted*
3 Tbsp. finely shredded Parmesan cheese
2 cloves garlic, smashed
¼ cup olive oil
Salt and black pepper

1. Remove 1 teaspoon zest and 3 tablespoons juice from lemon. In a food processor combine spinach, almonds, Parmesan cheese, lemon zest and juice, and garlic. Cover and pulse until chopped. With the motor running, add olive oil in a steady stream until combined. Season to taste with salt and pepper. Makes about 1 cup (16 servings).
*Tip To toast nuts, spread in a shallow baking pan. Bake in a 350°F oven 5 to 10 minutes or until golden, stirring pan once or twice and watching closely to prevent burning.
PER SERVING *278 cal., 24 g fat (4 g sat. fat), 188 mg chol., 223 mg sodium, 7 g carb., 3 g fiber, 2 g sugars, 11 g pro.*

CHUNKY CRANBERRY RELISH

START TO FINISH 20 minutes

1 cup full-bodied red wine (such as Pinot Noir) or cranberry juice
1½ cups sugar
¼ tsp. salt
1 cinnamon stick
6 cups fresh cranberries, washed and drained
1 Tbsp. orange zest

1. In a stainless-steel skillet combine wine, sugar, salt, and cinnamon. Bring to a simmer over medium heat, stirring to dissolve sugar. Cook 1 minute. Add the cranberries and bring to boiling; reduce heat. Boil gently over medium-high heat 3 to 5 minutes or until skins pop*, stirring occasionally. Stir in the orange zest.

2. Cool completely; discard cinnamon. If desired, for a thicker relish crush berries slightly with the back of a spoon. Cover and store in the refrigerator up to 1 week. Makes 4 to 5 cups (8 servings).
*Tip For softer, smoother cranberry sauce, prepare as directed, except boil gently 20 minutes.
PER SERVING *94 cal., 0 fat, 0 mg chol., 33 mg sodium, 22 g carb., 2 g fiber, 18 g sugars, 0 g pro.*

TRIPLE-OLIVE TAPENADE

START TO FINISH 20 minutes

1½ cups pitted green olives
1½ cups pitted Kalamata olives
½ cup pitted oil-cured black olives
⅓ cup olive oil
2 Tbsp. capers, drained
2 Tbsp. balsamic vinegar
1 Tbsp. Dijon mustard
2 anchovy fillets (optional)
2 cloves garlic, minced
1 Tbsp. snipped fresh basil, thyme, oregano, parsley, and/or rosemary

1. In a food processor or blender combine the first nine ingredients (through garlic). Cover and pulse until finely chopped, stopping to scrape down sides as necessary. Stir in fresh herb(s). Makes 3 cups (48 servings).
PER SERVING *29 cal., 3 g fat (0 g sat. fat), 0 mg chol., 146 mg sodium, 1 g carb., 0 g fiber, 0 g sugars, 0 g pro.*
Orange-Scented Almond Tapenade Prepare as directed, except substitute 1 cup toasted slivered almonds for the green olives. Add 1 tablespoon orange zest and 2 tablespoons orange juice to the mixture before processing.

EASY SESAME DINNER ROLLS

PREP 20 minutes
RISE 45 minutes
BAKE 25 minutes at 375°F

1 16-oz. loaf frozen white or wheat bread dough
¼ cup sesame seeds
2 Tbsp. yellow cornmeal
2 Tbsp. grated Parmesan cheese
1 tsp. salt-free lemon pepper seasoning
3 Tbsp. butter, melted

1. Thaw dough according to package directions. Grease a 9×9-inch baking pan; set aside. In a shallow dish or small bowl stir together sesame seeds, cornmeal, Parmesan cheese, and lemon-pepper seasoning. Place butter in a second dish. Cut the dough into 16 equal pieces. Shape each piece into a ball by pulling and pinching dough underneath. Roll dough pieces in butter, then in the sesame seed mixture to lightly coat. Arrange dough pieces, smooth sides up, in the prepared pan.

2. Cover pan with waxed paper and let rise in a warm place until nearly double in size (45 to 60 minutes).

3. Preheat oven to 375°F. Bake 25 minutes or until golden brown. Transfer rolls to a wire rack. Cool slightly before serving. Makes 16 servings.
PER SERVING *109 cal., 4 g fat (2 g sat. fat), 6 mg chol., 180 mg sodium, 15 g carb., 1 g fiber, 1 g sugars, 2 g pro.*
Garlic-Herb Rolls Prepare as directed except omit lemon-pepper seasoning and add 1 teaspoon dried Italian seasoning, crushed, and ½ teaspoon garlic powder to sesame seed mixture.

EASY SESAME
DINNER ROLLS

PAELLA-STYLE
STUFFING

PAELLA-STYLE STUFFING

PREP 30 minutes
BAKE 25 minutes at 350°F

2	Tbsp. canola oil
⅓	cup chopped onion
3	cloves garlic, minced
⅔	cup short grain rice
1⅓	cups reduced-sodium chicken broth
¼	tsp. saffron threads
6	oz. cooked, smoked chorizo sausage, diced
¾	cup chopped red sweet pepper
½	cup thinly sliced celery
2	Tbsp. snipped fresh parsley
¼	tsp. salt
¼	tsp. black pepper
6	cups dried French bread cubes*
½	cup sliced pimiento-stuffed green olives
1¼ to 1½	cups reduced-sodium chicken broth

1. Preheat oven to 350°F. Lightly grease a 2-quart baking dish. In a small saucepan heat 1 tablespoon of the oil over medium-high heat. Add onion; cook and stir 3 minutes or until onion is tender. Add garlic; cook and stir 30 seconds. Add rice, stirring 3 minutes or just until rice starts to brown. Carefully add the 1⅓ cups broth and the saffron threads. Bring to boiling; reduce heat. Cook, covered, 15 minutes or until rice is cooked and liquid is absorbed.
2. Meanwhile, in a large skillet heat the remaining 1 tablespoon oil. Add chorizo, sweet pepper, and celery; cook and stir 4 minutes or until chorizo begins to brown and vegetables are tender. Remove from heat. Add rice mixture, parsley, salt, and black pepper to skillet; toss to combine.
3. In a large bowl combine rice mixture, bread cubes, and olives. Toss to combine. Drizzle with the 1¼ cups broth to moisten, tossing to combine. Spoon stuffing into prepared dish. Cover with foil. Bake 25 to 30 minutes or until heated through. Makes 6 servings.
*Tip To make dry bread cubes, preheat oven to 300°F. Cut 8 oz. French bread into ¾-inch cubes (6 cups). Spread into a 15×10-inch baking pan. Bake 10 to 15 minutes or until dry, stirring twice; cool. (Cubes will continue to dry as they cool.)
PER SERVING *408 cal., 19 g fat (5 g sat. fat), 240 mg chol., 1,067 mg sodium, 43 g carb., 3 g fiber, 3 g sugars, 15 g pro.*

POTATOES WITH GARDEN CONFETTI

PREP 35 minutes
BAKE 45 minutes at 425°F +2 hours at 325°F
CHILL 2 hours

	Nonstick cooking spray
5	lb. red-skin potatoes
1	8-oz. pkg. regular or reduced-fat cream cheese, cut up and softened
1	tsp. salt
1	tsp. cracked black pepper
1½	cups half-and-half
1	recipe Garden Confetti
2	Tbsp. butter, melted

1. Preheat oven to 425°F. Coat a 9×13-inch baking dish with cooking spray. Prick potatoes with a fork and place in pan. Bake 45 to 60 minutes or until tender. Reduce oven temperature to 325°F.
2. In batches, in an extra-large bowl, mash potatoes until slightly lumpy.
3. Return all the potatoes to the extra-large bowl; add cream cheese, salt, and pepper. Gradually beat in half-and-half until mashed potatoes are light and fluffy. Transfer mashed potatoes to the prepared dish. Top with Garden Confetti; drizzle with melted butter.
4. Bake, covered, 1 hour. Bake, uncovered, 1 to 1¼ hours more or until heated through. Makes 10 servings.
Garden Confetti In a large skillet melt 3 tablespoons butter over medium-high heat. Add 1½ cups shredded carrots; 1 medium onion, halved and thinly sliced; ½ cup each finely chopped red sweet pepper and green sweet pepper; and 2 cloves garlic, minced. Cook and stir 4 to 5 minutes or until vegetables are tender. If desired, stir in 1 teaspoon snipped fresh rosemary or thyme.
PER SERVING *350 cal., 18 g fat (11 g sat. fat), 51 mg chol., 426 mg sodium, 43 g carb., 5 g fiber, 7 g sugars, 7 g pro.*

CELERY ROOT SOUP WITH PARSLEY OIL

PREP 25 minutes
COOK 25 minutes

- 4   cups chicken broth
- ½   medium celery root (about 10 oz.), peeled and cut into 1-inch pieces
- 2   medium russet potatoes (about 12 oz.), peeled and cut into 1-inch pieces
- ½   cup lightly packed fresh parsley leaves
- ¼   cup olive oil
      Salt
- 1   tsp. lemon juice
      Black pepper

1. In a large saucepan combine broth, celery root, and potatoes. Bring to boiling; reduce heat. Simmer, covered, 25 to 30 minutes or until vegetables are very tender. Remove from heat; cool slightly.

2. Meanwhile, for Parsley Oil, in a food processor or blender combine the ½ cup parsley, the oil, and a pinch of salt. Cover and process or blend until well mixed (parsley will still be in small pieces). Press mixture firmly through a strainer into a small bowl; discard parsley.

3. Transfer half the celery root-potato mixture to the food processor or blender. Cover and process or blend until smooth. Repeat with the remaining celery root-potato mixture. Return all the soup to the saucepan. Stir in lemon juice; heat through. Season to taste with additional salt and pepper. Ladle soup into bowls. Drizzle with the parsley oil. If desired, top with additional parsley. Makes 4 servings.

PER SERVING *228 cal., 14 g fat (2 g sat. fat), 5 mg chol., 1,123 mg sodium, 23 g carb., 3 g fiber, 3 g sugars, 4 g pro.*

COCONUT ACORN SQUASH AND CARROT SOUP

PREP 25 minutes
BAKE 40 minutes at 400°F
COOK 15 minutes

- 1   medium acorn squash*
- 1   Tbsp. butter
- 1   cup shredded carrot
- ½   cup chopped sweet onion
- 1   Tbsp. grated fresh ginger
- 1   13- to 14-oz. can unsweetened coconut milk
- 1½   cups water
- ½   tsp. salt
       Basil leaves and/or toasted squash seeds (optional)

1. Preheat oven to 400°F. Cut squash in half lengthwise; remove seeds. Arrange squash halves, cut sides down, in a shallow foil-lined baking pan. Bake, uncovered, 40 minutes or until tender. Scoop flesh from squash; discard skin.

2. In a large saucepan melt butter over medium heat. Add carrot, onion, and ginger. Cook and stir 3 to 4 minutes or until tender. Add squash flesh, coconut milk, water, and salt. Bring to boiling; reduce heat. Simmer, covered, 10 minutes, stirring occasionally.

3. Use an immersion blender to puree the soup (or transfer to a blender). Ladle into bowls and, if desired, top with basil leaves and/or toasted squash seeds. Makes 4 servings.

Toasted Squash Seeds Rinse seeds and pat dry with paper towels. In a bowl mix seeds with ½ teaspoon vegetable oil. Spread seeds in a single layer in a shallow baking pan. Sprinkle lightly with salt. Roast in a 400°F oven 5 to 8 minutes until toasted, stirring once.

*Tip To microwave squash instead of baking, pierce squash in 3 places with a sharp knife. Microwave 7 minutes or until tender. When cool enough to handle, slice squash in half and remove seeds. Reserve some of the seeds for garnish, if desired. Scoop flesh from squash halves and set aside. Discard skins.

PER SERVING *252 cal., 18 g fat (16 g sat. fat), 8 mg chol., 388 mg sodium, 20 g carb., 3 g fiber, 2 g sugars, 2 g pro.*

CELERY ROOT SOUP WITH PARSLEY OIL

COCONUT ACORN
SQUASH AND
CARROT SOUP

CORN PUDDING
CASSEROLE

CORN PUDDING CASSEROLE

PREP 30 minutes
BAKE 50 minutes at 350°F
STAND 15 minutes

- 6 dried tomatoes (not oil-pack)
- ½ cup chopped onion
- 2 cloves garlic, minced
- 2 Tbsp. butter
- 1¼ cups shredded zucchini
- 1 16-oz. pkg. frozen whole kernel corn, thawed
- 6 eggs, lightly beaten
- 3 cups whole milk
- ¾ cup yellow cornmeal
- 1 15-oz. carton whole milk ricotta cheese
- 2 tsp. dried Italian seasoning, crushed
- 1 tsp. salt
- ¼ tsp. black pepper
- 1 cup finely shredded Parmesan cheese (4 oz.)
- 1 cup panko
- 1 Tbsp. butter, melted
  Fresh Italian parsley (optional)

1. Preheat oven to 350°F. Grease a 3-quart baking dish; set aside. In a small bowl cover tomatoes with boiling water. Let stand 15 minutes; drain. Chop tomatoes; set aside.

2. Meanwhile, in a large skillet cook onion and garlic in 2 tablespoons hot butter over medium heat 4 minutes or until tender. Add zucchini; cook 2 minutes more. Stir in corn and chopped tomatoes; set aside.

3. In a large bowl whisk together eggs and milk. Gradually whisk in cornmeal. Whisk in ricotta cheese, Italian seasoning, salt, and pepper. Stir in the corn mixture and Parmesan cheese. Carefully pour into prepared dish (dish will be full).

4. Bake 20 minutes. Meanwhile, in a bowl toss together panko and 1 tablespoon melted butter. Sprinkle on casserole. Bake 30 minutes or until the top is brown and a knife inserted into the center comes out clean. If desired, sprinkle with parsley. Makes 12 servings.

Make-Ahead Directions Prepare as directed, except do not preheat oven and after Step 2 cool zucchini mixture to room temperature. Once cool, continue with Step 3 and pour into prepared baking dish. Cover tightly with foil; chill up to 24 hours. Stir corn pudding before baking. Bake and top as directed in Step 4.

CRISPY PARMESAN-ROASTED BUTTERNUT SQUASH

PER SERVING *279 cal., 14 g fat (8 g sat. fat), 142 mg chol., 455 mg sodium, 24 g carb., 2 g fiber, 6 g sugars, 15 g pro.*

CRISPY PARMESAN-ROASTED BUTTERNUT SQUASH

PREP 20 minutes
ROAST 25 minutes at 425°F

- Nonstick cooking spray
- 1 1½- to 1¾-lb. butternut squash, peeled, seeded, and cut into ¾-inch pieces
- 2 Tbsp. olive oil
- ½ tsp. kosher salt
- ⅛ tsp. black pepper
- ⅓ cup grated Parmesan cheese
- ¼ tsp. dried thyme, sage, or basil, crushed

1. Preheat oven to 425°F. Coat a 15×10-inch baking pan with cooking spray. Place squash in prepared pan. Drizzle with oil and sprinkle with salt and pepper; toss to coat.

2. Roast 15 minutes. Stir squash; roast 5 minutes more. Stir in cheese and thyme. Roast 5 minutes or until squash is tender. Makes 4 servings.

PER SERVING *154 cal., 9 g fat (2 g sat. fat), 6 mg chol., 267 mg sodium, 18 g carb., 3 g fiber, 3 g sugars, 3 g pro.*

NUTS AND BERRIES
WINTER SLAW

NUTS AND BERRIES WINTER SLAW

PREP 30 minutes
CHILL 1 hour

1	navel orange
3	Tbsp. packed brown sugar
½	tsp. kosher salt
½	clove garlic, crushed
⅛	tsp. curry powder
⅛	tsp. cracked black pepper
½	cup fresh cranberries
3	Tbsp. coarsely chopped red onion
1	Tbsp. honey
2	tsp. canola oil
¾	lb. Brussels sprouts, trimmed and thinly sliced, or purchased shaved Brussels sprouts (about 3 cups)
3	Tbsp. toasted hazelnuts, coarsely chopped

1. For dressing, with a vegetable peeler, remove a wide, 2-inch-long strip of peel from the orange. Peel and segment orange. In a food processor combine orange peel strip, brown sugar, salt, garlic, curry powder, and pepper. Pulse until peel is finely chopped. Add cranberries and onion; pulse until cranberries are chopped. Add orange segments and pulse to chop. Transfer to a bowl; stir in honey and oil. (Dressing can be covered and chilled up to 24 hours.)
2. In a bowl combine Brussels sprouts and dressing. Cover and chill 1 to 24 hours before serving. To serve, stir and sprinkle with hazelnuts. Makes 10 servings.
PER SERVING *62 cal., 2 g fat (0 g sat. fat), 0 mg chol., 107 mg sodium, 10 g carb., 2 g fiber, 7 g sugars, 1 g pro.*

ROASTED CAULIFLOWER WITH CRANBERRIES

PREP 15 minutes
ROAST 25 minutes at 450°F

8	cups cauliflower florets
1	large red or yellow sweet onion, cut into wedges
3	Tbsp. olive oil
1	tsp. kosher salt
1½	cups fresh or frozen cranberries
¼	cup balsamic vinegar
¼	cup honey
¼	tsp. cracked black pepper
1	Tbsp. snipped fresh thyme

1. Preheat oven to 450°F. Place cauliflower and onion in a shallow baking pan. Drizzle with oil and sprinkle with

½ teaspoon of the salt; toss to coat. Roast 15 minutes. Stir in cranberries. Roast 10 to 15 minutes more or until cauliflower and onion are tender.

2. Meanwhile, in a small saucepan combine vinegar, honey, pepper, and remaining ½ teaspoon salt. Simmer 10 minutes or until sightly thickened, stirring occasionally.

3. Toss cauliflower mixture with vinegar mixture. Sprinkle with thyme. Makes 8 servings.

PER SERVING *135 cal., 5 g fat (1 g sat. fat), 0 mg chol., 281 mg sodium, 21 g carb., 4 g fiber, 14 g sugars, 3 g pro.*

OVEN-ROASTED BRUSSELS SPROUTS WITH APPLES, CHERRIES, AND PECANS

PREP 10 minutes
ROAST 20 minutes at 425°F

1   lb. Brussels sprouts
2   Tbsp. olive oil
½   tsp. kosher salt
⅛   tsp. cayenne pepper
1   cup sliced or coarsely chopped apple
½   cup dried cherries or cranberries
¼   cup chopped pecans
¼   cup bottled red wine vinaigrette or other vinaigrette

1. Preheat oven to 425°F. Line a 15×10-inch baking pan with foil. Trim stems and remove any wilted outer leaves from Brussels sprouts. Halve sprouts lengthwise.

2. Place Brussels sprouts in the prepared pan. Drizzle with oil and sprinkle with salt and cayenne pepper; toss to combine.

3. Roast, uncovered, 15 minutes. Stir in apple, dried cherries, and pecans. Roast, uncovered, 5 to 10 minutes more or until sprouts are crisp-tender and lightly browned. Drizzle with vinaigrette; toss gently to coat. Makes 4 servings.

PER SERVING *250 cal., 15 g fat (2 g sat. fat), 0 mg chol., 389 mg sodium, 32 g carb., 6 g fiber, 18 g sugars, 5 g pro.*

ROASTED CAULIFLOWER WITH CRANBERRIES

OVEN-ROASTED BRUSSELS SPROUTS WITH APPLES, CHERRIES, AND PECANS

PEAS WITH MUSHROOMS, SHALLOTS, AND RED SWEET PEPPER

START TO FINISH 30 minutes

2   Tbsp. butter
8   oz. whole fresh button or cremini mushrooms, quartered
¾   cup chopped red sweet pepper
¼   cup coarsely chopped shallots
1   16-oz. pkg. frozen petite peas, thawed
¼   tsp. salt
¼   tsp. black pepper
1   Tbsp. snipped fresh tarragon or mint
2   tsp. lemon zest

1. In a large skillet melt the butter over medium heat. Add the mushrooms, sweet pepper, and shallots; cook 5 minutes or until tender but not brown, stirring occasionally. Stir in the peas, salt, and pepper. Cook 5 minutes or until peas are tender, stirring occasionally. Stir in tarragon. Transfer to a serving bowl. Sprinkle with lemon zest. Makes 8 servings.

PER SERVING *86 cal., 3 g fat (2 g sat. fat), 8 mg chol., 231 mg sodium, 11 g carb., 3 g fiber, 4 g sugars, 4 g pro.*

BACON AND PEAR AUTUMN SALAD

START TO FINISH 25 minutes

8   slices smoked peppered bacon
1   Tbsp. extra-virgin olive oil
2   shallots, thinly sliced
    Kosher salt and freshly ground black pepper
2   Tbsp. red wine vinegar
6   cups torn fresh kale, Swiss chard, and/or beet greens
1   cup cooked, cooled grains, such as barley or farro
2   bosc pears, cored and thinly sliced
4   oz. Gouda cheese, cubed

1. In a large skillet cook bacon until crisp; remove to paper towels to drain, reserving 1 tablespoon drippings in skillet. Add the olive oil to skillet; add shallots and a pinch of salt. Cook over medium heat 3 to 4 minutes or until shallots are soft and golden brown, stirring occasionally. Stir in vinegar; remove from heat. Scrape up browned bits from bottom of skillet.

2. Place greens in a large bowl. Pour warm dressing over; toss to coat. Season to taste with salt and pepper. Cut bacon into 1-inch pieces. Add bacon, grains, and pears to greens mixture; toss to coat. Top with cheese. Makes 6 servings.

PER SERVING *257 cal., 14 g fat (6 g sat. fat), 34 mg chol., 421 mg sodium, 23 g carb., 5 g fiber, 8 g sugars, 12 g pro.*

PEAS WITH MUSHROOMS, SHALLOTS, AND RED SWEET PEPPER

**BACON AND PEAR
AUTUMN SALAD**

ORANGE- AND
BALSAMIC-GLAZED
TRICOLOR CARROTS

ORANGE- AND BALSAMIC-GLAZED TRICOLOR CARROTS

PREP 25 minutes
COOK 15 minutes

2   lb. medium red, yellow, and/or orange carrots, peeled
½   cup orange juice
¼   cup balsamic vinegar
4   tsp. sugar
¾   tsp. salt
¼   tsp. black pepper
2   Tbsp. butter
1   Tbsp. snipped fresh chives

1. Place a steamer basket in a large saucepan. Add water to just below the bottom of the basket. Bring water to boiling. Add carrots to steamer basket. Cover and reduce heat. Steam 15 to 20 minutes or just until tender. Transfer the carrots to a serving platter; cover and keep warm.
2. Meanwhile, for glaze, in a medium saucepan combine orange juice, balsamic vinegar, sugar, salt, and pepper. Bring to boiling; reduce heat. Simmer, uncovered, 12 minutes or until reduced to a syrupy consistency (about ⅓ cup). Stir in butter.
3. Drizzle glaze over carrots and sprinkle with chives. Makes 6 servings.
PER SERVING *126 cal., 4 g fat (2 g sat. fat), 10 mg chol., 432 mg sodium, 21 g carb., 4 g fiber, 13 g sugars, 2 g pro.*

SHAVED CELERY AND MUSHROOM SALAD WITH PECORINO

START TO FINISH 35 minutes

4   cups thinly bias-sliced celery
4   cups thinly sliced fresh cremini mushrooms
½   cup coarsely snipped fresh parsley
¼   cup olive oil
3   to 4 Tbsp. lemon juice
2   Tbsp. white wine vinegar
1   tsp. kosher salt
2   oz. Pecorino Romano cheese, shaved

1. In an extra-large bowl combine celery, mushrooms, and parsley. For dressing, in a screw-top jar combine olive oil, lemon juice, and vinegar. Cover and shake well.
2. Drizzle dressing over celery mixture and sprinkle with salt; toss gently to coat. Top with cheese. Makes 6 servings.
To Make Ahead Prepare as directed through Step 1. Cover and chill up to 24 hours. Continue as directed.

PER SERVING *146 cal., 12 g fat (3 g sat. fat), 10 mg chol., 561 mg sodium, 5 g carb., 2 g fiber, 3 g sugars, 6 g pro.*

SHAVED CELERY AND MUSHROOM SALAD WITH PECORINO

Bites and Sips

Savory bites that are casual and carefree are the best party food. Guests can nibble on these appetizers—dips, meatballs, wings, and nachos—while mixing and mingling. Add a tasty sipper and let the celebration begin.

SPICY GLAZED RIBS, PAGE 35

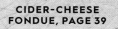

CIDER-CHEESE
FONDUE, PAGE 39

PROSCIUTTO-WRAPPED HONEY-LEMON SHRIMP

PROSCIUTTO-WRAPPED HONEY-LEMON SHRIMP

PREP 40 minutes
BROIL 4 minutes

24 fresh or frozen jumbo shrimp in shells (about 1 lb.)
1   lemon
2   Tbsp. honey
2   tsp. snipped fresh parsley
6   very thin slices prosciutto (4 to 5 oz.)

1. Thaw shrimp, if frozen. Preheat broiler. Peel and devein shrimp, leaving tails intact. Rinse shrimp; pat dry with paper towels. Place shrimp in a large bowl. Remove ½ teaspoon zest and 2 tablespoons juice from lemon. In a small bowl combine lemon zest and juice, the honey, and parsley. Pour over shrimp; toss gently to coat.
2. Cut prosciutto slices in half crosswise then in half lengthwise (24 pieces total). Wrap a piece of prosciutto around each shrimp; if necessary secure with a wooden toothpick.
3. Place shrimp on the lightly greased unheated rack of a broiler pan. Broil 4 to 5 inches from heat 4 to 6 minutes or until shrimp are opaque and prosciutto is crisp, turning once.
4. If desired, sprinkle shrimp with additional lemon zest and snipped fresh parsley, and drizzle with additional honey. Makes 8 servings.
PER SERVING *84 cal., 4 g fat (0 g sat. fat), 32 mg chol., 283 mg sodium, 5 g carb., 0 g fiber, 4 g sugars, 8 g pro.*

GREEK STUFFED TURKEY ROULADE

PREP 35 minutes
ROAST 30 minutes at 400°F
STAND 10 minutes

2   12- to 14-oz. turkey breast tenderloins
½   tsp. salt
¼   tsp. black pepper
1   cup chopped roasted yellow sweet peppers*
½   cup crumbled feta cheese (2 oz.)
¼   cup oil-pack dried tomatoes, drained and chopped
¼   cup snipped fresh basil

GREEK STUFFED TURKEY ROULADE

2   tsp. snipped fresh thyme
3   cloves garlic, minced
1   Tbsp. olive oil
    Salt and black pepper
    Fresh basil leaves (optional)

1. Preheat oven to 400°F. Line a 15×10-inch baking pan with foil. Place a rack in the foil-lined pan. Make a lengthwise cut along the center of each turkey tenderloin, cutting almost to but not through the other side. Spread open. Using a meat mallet, flatten each tenderloin between two pieces of plastic wrap to about ¼-inch thickness. Sprinkle turkey portions with the ½ teaspoon salt and the ¼ teaspoon pepper.
2. For stuffing, in a medium bowl combine roasted yellow peppers, cheese, dried tomatoes, the snipped basil, thyme, and garlic.
3. Spread stuffing on turkey portions to within ½ inch of edges. Starting from a long side, roll up each portion into a spiral. Tie at 2-inch intervals with 100-percent-cotton kitchen string. Brush rolls with oil and sprinkle with additional salt and pepper. Place rolls on the rack in the prepared baking pan.

4. Roast, uncovered, 30 to 35 minutes or until turkey is no longer pink (170°F). Cover loosely with foil; let stand 10 minutes before slicing. Remove string. Cut rolls into 1-inch slices. Serve warm. If desired, serve on basil leaves. Makes 20 servings.
Make-Ahead Prepare as directed, except do not slice turkey rolls. Wrap each roll in plastic wrap and chill up to 48 hours. Cut into 1-inch slices before serving.
*Tip To roast yellow sweet peppers, preheat oven to 425°F. Quarter 2 yellow sweet peppers lengthwise; remove and discard stems, seeds, and membranes. Place pepper quarters, cut sides down, on a foil-lined baking sheet. Roast 20 to 25 minutes or until pepper skins are blistered and dark. Bring foil up around peppers to enclose. Let stand 15 minutes or until cool. Using a sharp knife, loosen edges of the skins; gently pull off the skin in strips and discard. Chop enough roasted peppers to equal 1 cup.
PER SERVING *59 cal., 2 g fat (1 g sat. fat), 24 mg chol., 146 mg sodium, 1 g carb., 0 g fiber, 0 g sugars, 9 g pro.*

TOASTED CRAB SANDWICHES

PREP 20 minutes
BROIL 1 minute
COOK 6 minutes

1   8-oz. container refrigerated lump
     crabmeat
2   Tbsp. mayonnaise
2   Tbsp. sour cream
2   Tbsp. chopped green onion
1   Tbsp. snipped fresh dill weed
2   tsp. lemon juice
3   Tbsp. butter, softened
⅛   tsp. cayenne pepper
4   English muffins, split
4   slices Swiss cheese

1. Preheat broiler. In a medium bowl combine crabmeat, mayonnaise, sour cream, green onion, dill, and lemon juice; set aside. In a small bowl combine butter and cayenne pepper.
2. Generously spread outsides of English muffin halves with butter mixture. Place four of the muffin halves, buttered sides down, on a baking sheet. Top with cheese. Broil 4 to 5 inches from heat 1 for to 2 minutes or until cheese starts to melt.
3. Spoon crab mixture onto cheese-topped muffin halves, spreading to edges. Top with remaining muffin halves, buttered sides up.
4. Heat a large griddle or skillet over medium heat. Add sandwiches; cook 6 minutes or until muffins are golden brown, turning once. Cut each sandwich into four portions. Makes 16 servings.
PER SERVING 108 cal., 6 g fat (3 g sat. fat), 21 mg chol., 252 mg sodium, 7 g carb., 0 g fiber, 1 g sugars, 6 g pro.

TOASTED CRAB SANDWICHES

MANGO-SRIRACHA WINGS

START TO FINISH 40 minutes

12   chicken wings (about 2½ lb.)
2   Tbsp. vegetable oil
1   medium mango, seeded, peeled,
     and cut up
½   14-oz. can unsweetened light
     coconut milk*
1   Tbsp. sriracha
1   Tbsp. fresh lime juice
1   tsp. kosher salt
     Thinly sliced green onions
     (optional)

1. Cut off and discard tips of chicken wings. Cut wings at joints to form 24 pieces. In an extra-large skillet heat oil over medium-high heat. Add wings; cook 10 minutes or until browned, turning once. Drain off fat.
2. In a food processor or blender process or blend mango until smooth. Transfer mango to a small bow; add coconut milk, sriracha, lime juice, and salt. Pour wing sauce over chicken wings. Simmer, covered, 5 minutes. Simmer, uncovered, 10 to 15 minutes more or until chicken is no longer pink and sauce is slightly thickened, stirring occasionally. Transfer to a serving platter. If desired, sprinkle with green onions. Makes 12 servings.
***** Thoroughly stir coconut milk before measuring.
PER SERVING 154 cal., 11 g fat (3 g sat. fat), 39 mg chol., 176 mg sodium, 3 g carb., 0 g fiber, 3 g sugars, 10 g pro.

LAMB MEATBALLS WITH CRANBERRY DRIZZLE

PREP 35 minutes
BAKE 15 minutes at 300°F

1   egg, lightly beaten
1   cup panko bread crumbs
¼   cup snipped fresh mint
3   cloves garlic, minced
½   tsp. salt
¼   tsp. black pepper
1   lb. ground lamb
1   lb. lean ground beef
1   16-oz. bottle cranberry juice
1   Tbsp. packed brown sugar
3   Tbsp. olive oil
    Toasted pita wedges (optional)
    Mint leaves (optional)

1. Preheat oven to 300°F. In a large bowl combine egg, panko, the ¼ cup mint, garlic, salt, and pepper. Add lamb and beef; mix well. Shape into 32 meatballs; set aside.
2. In a medium saucepan bring cranberry juice to boiling; reduce heat. Simmer 25 to 30 minutes or until reduced to ½ cup. Add brown sugar. Stir until sugar is dissolved.
3. Meanwhile, in an extra-large skillet heat olive oil over medium heat. Brown half of the meatballs at a time in hot oil, turning to brown evenly. Place meatballs in a single layer in a 15×10×1-inch baking pan. Bake, uncovered, 15 to 20 minutes or until done (160°F).
4. Add cranberry mixture to the skillet. Bring to boiling; reduce heat. Simmer 3 to 5 minutes or until mixture thickens to syrupy consistency. Add meatballs and stir to coat.
5. Arrange meatballs on a serving plate; drizzle with cranberry sauce. If desired, serve with Toasted Pita Wedges and sprinkle with fresh mint. Makes 32 servings.
PER SERVING *101 cal., 7 g fat (3 g sat. fat), 27 mg chol., 62 mg sodium, 4 g carb., 0 g fiber, 0 g sugars, 5 g pro.*
Toasted Pita Wedges Preheat oven to 350°F. Cut a pita bread round into 6 wedges and split each wedge in half horizontally. Brush wedges with 1 tablespoon olive oil; sprinkle with salt and pepper. Bake wedges on a baking sheet 5 to 8 minutes or until golden brown.

LAMB MEATBALLS
WITH CRANBERRY
DRIZZLE

SPICY
GLAZED
RIBS

SPICY GLAZED RIBS

PREP 15 minutes
BAKE 1 hour 30 minutes at 350°F

2   lb. pork loin back ribs or meaty pork spareribs, cut into single-rib portions
1   orange
1   8-oz. jar hoisin sauce
½   cup sugar
½   cup soy sauce
½   cup tomato paste
¼   cup sweet rice wine (mirin) or sweet white wine
¼   cup bottled minced garlic
1   Tbsp. bottled hot pepper sauce
    Sliced green onions (optional)
    Sesame seeds (optional)

1. Preheat oven to 350°F. Place ribs in a large shallow roasting pan. Bake 45 minutes. Carefully drain off fat.
2. Meanwhile, for sauce, remove 1 teaspoon zest and 2 tablespoons juice from orange. In a bowl combine the remaining ingredients except onions and seeds.
3. Pour sauce over ribs; stir to coat. Bake 45 minutes more or until ribs are tender, stirring every 10 minutes. If desired, sprinkle ribs with sliced green onions and sesame seeds. Makes 12 servings.
PER SERVING *234 cal., 10 g fat (3 g sat. fat), 37 mg chol., 1,028 mg sodium, 24 g carb., 1 g fiber, 18 g sugars, 10 g pro.*

GYRO NACHOS WITH TZATZIKI SAUCE

PREP 30 minutes
SLOW COOK 6 hours (low) or 3 hours (high)

2   lb. bone-in chicken thighs, skinned
1   red onion, thinly sliced
2   Tbsp. lemon juice
2   Tbsp. red wine vinegar
2   Tbsp. olive oil
6   cloves garlic, minced
4   tsp. dried oregano, crushed
1   tsp. salt
1   8-oz. bag plain pita chips
1   recipe Tzatziki Sauce
½   cup chopped tomato
½   cup sliced Kalamata olives
    Fresh dill

1. Place first eight ingredients (through salt) in a 3½- or 4-quart slow cooker. Cover and cook on low 6 to 7 hours or on high 3 to 3½ hours.

GYRO NACHOS WITH TZATZIKI SAUCE

2. Remove chicken and onion from cooker using a slotted spoon. When chicken is cool enough to handle, remove bones. Shred chicken using two forks. In a bowl combine chicken and onion; add enough cooking liquid to moisten.
3. Spoon chicken on a platter of pita chips. Top with Tzatziki Sauce, tomato, olives, and fresh dill. Makes 10 servings.

Tzatziki Sauce In a small bowl combine 1 6-oz. carton plain Greek yogurt, 1 cup chopped cucumber, 2 teaspoons snipped fresh dill, 2 cloves minced garlic, 1 teaspoon lemon juice, and ¼ teaspoon salt. Makes 1⅓ cups sauce.
PER SERVING *219 cal., 9 g fat (1 g sat. fat), 52 mg chol., 499 mg sodium, 19 g carb., 2 g fiber, 2 g sugars, 15 g pro.*

SAVORY WALNUTS

ROSEMARY-ROASTED CHICKPEAS

SAVORY WALNUTS

BAKE 12 minutes at 350°F
PREP 10 minutes

2   cups walnut halves
2   Tbsp. Worcestershire-style
     marinade for chicken
1   Tbsp. olive oil
2   tsp. snipped fresh thyme or ½ tsp.
     dried thyme, crushed
1   tsp. snipped fresh rosemary or
     ¼ tsp. dried rosemary, crushed
¼   tsp. salt
⅛   tsp. cayenne pepper

1. Preheat oven to 350°F. Spread
walnuts in an even layer in a 13×9-inch
baking pan. In a small bowl combine the
remaining ingredients. Drizzle over nuts;
toss gently to coat.
2. Bake 12 to 15 minutes or until nuts are
toasted, stirring occasionally. Spread
nuts on a large sheet of foil; cool. Store in
an airtight container or resealable plastic
bag at room temperature up to 1 week.
Makes 8 servings.
PER SERVING *259 cal., 27 g fat
(4 g sat. fat), 0 mg chol., 191 mg sodium,
5 g carb., 3 g fiber, 0 g sugars, 3 g pro.*

ROSEMARY-ROASTED CHICKPEAS

PREP 10 minutes
ROAST 40 minutes at 425°F

2   15- to 16-oz. cans chickpeas
     (garbanzo beans), rinsed and well
     drained
3   Tbsp. olive oil
1   Tbsp. finely snipped fresh
     rosemary
1   Tbsp. honey
½   tsp. kosher salt
¼   tsp. cayenne pepper

1. Preheat oven to 425°F. In a 15×10-inch
baking pan combine chickpeas and
1 tablespoon of the oil. Roast 40 minutes
or until browned and crisp, stirring every
10 minutes (beans may pop).
2. Meanwhile, in a small bowl combine
the remaining oil and the remaining
ingredients. Drizzle over warm beans;
toss to coat. Let cool. If desired sprinkle
with additional finely chopped fresh
rosemary. Makes 9 servings.
PER SERVING *117 cal., 6 g fat (1 g sat. fat),
0 mg chol., 170 mg sodium, 14 g carb.,
3 g fiber, 4 g sugars, 4 g pro.*

Candied Chickpeas Prepare as directed
except preheat oven to 325°F and line
the baking pan with parchment paper.
Omit rosemary, honey, and cayenne
pepper. Place chickpeas in prepared
pan. Reduce olive oil to 1 tablespoon;
drizzle over chickpeas. Sprinkle with
¼ cup packed brown sugar, the salt, and
¼ teaspoon black pepper; toss to coat.
Roast 50 minutes or until deep golden
brown, stirring twice; cool. Store, covered,
in refrigerator up to 3 days.

CRISPY GREENS CHIPS

PREP 20 minutes
BAKE 20 minutes at 300°F

10   to 12 oz. fresh green curly kale,
     Swiss chard, mustard greens, or
     collard greens
1   Tbsp. olive oil
¼   tsp. salt
¼   tsp. smoked paprika or ground
     chipotle chile pepper

1. Preheat oven to 300°F. Thoroughly
wash and drain greens; pat dry with
paper towels. Remove and discard the
tough center stalks from leaves. Tear

leaves into 2- to 3-inch pieces (should have about 8 cups kale or collard green pieces, 6 cups Swiss chard pieces, or 10 cups mustard green pieces). In an extra-large bowl combine oil, salt, and smoked paprika. Add greens; toss to coat.

2. Place a wire rack on each of four baking sheets. Arrange greens in a single layer on the wire racks. Bake on separate oven racks, in batches if necessary, 20 minutes or until greens are crisp, rearranging baking sheets halfway through. (For a dehydrator, place leaves in a single layer on mesh-lined dehydrator trays. Dehydrate at 135°F for 2½ to 3 hours or until dry and brittle.)

3. Cool greens on wire racks. Transfer to an airtight storage container. Cover and seal. Store at room temperature 5 to 7 days. If chips begin to lose crispness, place on a baking sheet and crisp in a 325°F oven 2 to 3 minutes. Makes 6 servings.

PER SERVING *34 cal., 3 g fat (0 g sat. fat), 0 mg chol., 108 mg sodium, 3 g carb., 1 g fiber, 1 g sugars, 1 g pro.*

Spicy Asiago Greens Chips Prepare as directed, except substitute 2 tablespoons freshly grated Asiago cheese and ½ teaspoon crushed red pepper for the smoked paprika or ground chipotle chile pepper. Store in the refrigerator.

RIO GRANDE DIP

PREP 20 minutes
SLOW COOK 3 hours (low)

4   oz. uncooked Italian turkey sausage links, casings removed if present
¼   cup finely chopped onion
1   15-oz. can reduced-fat refried black beans
¾   cup shredded reduced-fat Monterey Jack cheese (3 oz.)
¾   cup bottled salsa
½   4-oz. can diced green chiles, undrained
2   Tbsp. shredded reduced-fat Monterey Jack cheese
1   9-oz. bag tortilla chips

1. In a medium skillet crumble sausage and cook with onion over medium-high heat until meat is browned, stirring to break up sausage as it cooks. Drain off fat. Transfer meat mixture to a 1½-quart slow cooker. Stir in refried beans, the ¾ cup cheese, salsa, and chiles.

2. Cover and cook on low 3 to 4 hours. If no heat setting is available, cook 3 to 4 hours.

3. Stir well before serving. Serve immediately or keep warm, covered, on warm- or low-heat setting up to 2 hours. Sprinkle dip with the 2 tablespoons cheese and serve with tortilla chips. Makes 24 servings.

PER SERVING *76 cal., 2 g fat (1 g sat. fat), 5 mg chol., 258 mg sodium, 12 g carb., 2 g fiber, 1 g sugars, 4 g pro.*

RIO GRANDE DIP

GARLICKY
SPINACH AND
FETA DIP

GARLICKY SPINACH AND FETA DIP

PREP 15 minutes
BAKE 20 minutes at 425°F

- 3   cloves garlic, minced
- 1   Tbsp. olive oil
- 10   oz. fresh arugula or spinach
- 8   oz. fresh spinach
- 1   8-oz. pkg. cream cheese, softened
- 1   cup plain Greek yogurt
- 1   cup mayonnaise
- ⅓   cup sliced pitted Kalamata olives
- ¼   tsp. black pepper
- 1   cup crumbled feta cheese (4 oz.)
- ½   cup chopped green onions
      Pita chips, multigrain snack crackers, and/or assorted cut-up vegetables

1. Preheat oven to 425°F. In a 4- to 6-quart Dutch oven cook and stir garlic in hot oil over medium heat for 1 minute. Gradually add arugula and spinach; cook and stir until greens are wilted. Drain well; cool slightly. Press out any excess liquid from greens. Using kitchen scissors, snip greens into bite-size pieces.
2. In a bowl combine greens, the next five ingredients (through pepper), ¾ cup of the feta, and ⅓ cup of the green onions. Transfer dip to a seasoned or greased 8- to 9-inch cast-iron skillet. Sprinkle with remaining ¼ cup feta cheese.
3. Bake 20 minutes or until heated through and bubbly around the edge. Sprinkle with remaining green onions. Serve dip with chips, crackers, and/or vegetables. Makes 32 servings.
PER SERVING *86 cal., 8 g fat (3 g sat. fat), 13 mg chol., 114 mg sodium, 1 g carb., 0 g fiber, 1 g sugars, 2 g pro.*

CIDER-CHEESE FONDUE (PHOTO, PAGE 29)

START TO FINISH 25 minutes

- 1   clove garlic, halved
- 1   12-oz. bottle hard cider
- 8   oz. Gruyère cheese, shredded
- 8   oz. Swiss cheese, shredded
- 8   oz. sharp cheddar cheese, shredded
- 2   Tbsp. cornstarch
- 2   tsp. bottled hot pepper sauce
      Dippers, such as fully cooked sausage, sourdough or pumpernickel bread cubes, and/or pear or apple wedges

CHAI-MAPLE CIDER

1. Rub garlic on the bottom and halfway up the sides of a large heavy saucepan; discard garlic.
2. Add hard cider to the saucepan and bring to a simmer over medium heat. In an extra-large bowl toss cheeses with cornstarch. A handful at a time, stir cheese into hard cider until melted and smooth. Stir in hot sauce.
3. Transfer to fondue pot and serve with assorted dippers. Makes 8 servings.
PER SERVING *407 cal., 27 g fat (16 g sat. fat), 86 mg chol., 507 mg sodium, 14 g carb., 0 g fiber, 2 g sugars, 24 g pro.*

CHAI-MAPLE CIDER

PREP 20 minutes
SLOW COOK 5 hours (low)
STAND 10 minutes

- 4   long strips orange peel*
- 2   to 3 cinnamon sticks
- 8   whole cloves
- 3   cardamom pods
- 25   whole black peppercorns
- 5   cups apple cider
- 1   cup water
- ½   cup pure maple syrup
- 8   black tea bags

1. For a spice bag, place the first five ingredients in the center of a double-thick, 6- to 8-inch square of 100%-cotton cheesecloth. Bring up corners; tie closed with clean kitchen string.
2. In a 3- to 4-quart slow cooker combine spice bag, apple cider, water, and syrup.
3. Cover; cook on low 5 to 6 hours. Add tea bags, draping strings over sides of cooker. Cover; let stand 10 minutes. Remove tea bags, gently pressing tea bags against sides of cooker to release liquid. Discard tea bags and spice bag. Ladle hot drink into mugs and, if desired, serve with an additional cinnamon stick and additional orange peel. Makes 8 servings.
* Use a vegetable peeler to remove the orange peel strips, avoiding any of the bitter white pith.
PER SERVING *128 cal., 0 g fat, 0 mg chol., 24 mg sodium, 32 g carb., 0 g fiber, 28 g sugars, 0 g pro.*

VIRGIN STRAWBERRY MOSCOW MULE

START TO FINISH 20 minutes

4   cups halved strawberries
6   cups diet ginger ale
¼   cup lime juice
    Crushed ice
½   cup loosely packed small fresh basil leaves
8   strawberries threaded on 8 bamboo skewers

1. In a blender or food processor combine strawberries, ½ cup of the ginger ale, and the lime juice. Cover and blend or process until smooth. Strain if desired.
2. Transfer strawberry mixture to a large pitcher. Slowly pour in the remaining ginger ale; stir gently. Fill eight glasses with crushed ice; divide basil and strawberry kabobs among glasses. Pour in strawberry mixture. Makes 8 servings.
PER SERVING *25 cal., 0 g fat, 0 mg chol., 61 mg sodium, 6 g carb., 1 g fiber, 4 g sugars, 1 g pro.*

LIMONCELLO

PREP 25 minutes
STAND 10 days
CHILL 8 hours

10   large lemons
1   750-ml. bottle vodka
3   cups sugar
2½   cups water
    Lemons, cut into wedges (optional)

1. Scrub 10 lemons with a vegetable brush. Using a vegetable peeler, carefully cut away enough yellow peel from the white pith to equal 2 cups. (If desired, juice lemons and reserve for another use.)
2. In a large glass pitcher or bowl combine the 2 cups lemon peel and vodka. Cover tightly and let stand in a cool, dry place 10 days, gently swirling the mixture in the pitcher each day. Strain through a fine-mesh sieve; discard lemon peel. Return to the pitcher.
3. For syrup, in a medium saucepan combine sugar and water. Bring just to boiling, stirring to dissolve sugar. Cool to room temperature.
4. Pour syrup into the lemon-infused vodka; stir to combine. Cover and chill 8 hours or overnight. Pour limoncello through a funnel into clean bottles; secure lids. Store in the refrigerator. Makes 56 servings.
PER SERVING *72 cal., 0 g fat, 0 mg chol., 1 mg sodium, 11 g carb., 0 g fiber, 11 g sugars, 0 g pro.*

LIMONCELLO COSMO

START TO FINISH 5 minutes

    Ice cubes
3   Tbsp. vodka
1   Tbsp. Limoncello, chilled
1   Tbsp. cranberry juice
    Fresh cranberries
    Lemon peel (optional)

1. Fill a cocktail shaker three-fourths full with ice. Add vodka, Limoncello, and cranberry juice. Cover and shake until the outside of the shaker becomes frosty. Strain into a chilled martini glass or other small glass. Top with fresh cranberries and, if desired, lemon peel. Makes 1 serving.
PER SERVING *146 cal., 0 g fat, 0 mg chol., 1 mg sodium, 7 g carb., 0 g fiber, 2 g sugars, 0 g pro.*

VIRGIN STRAWBERRY MOSCOW MULE

LIMONCELLO

LIMONCELLO
COSMO

BREAKFAST PIZZA,
PAGE 48

Hearty Brunch

During the holiday season, start the day in a celebratory style with an extra-special morning meal. Impress guests with these breakfast and brunch dishes, including a savory strata, breakfast pizza, home-baked doughnuts, and wake-me-up beverages.

BAGEL AND LOX
SKILLET STRATA

BAGEL AND LOX SKILLET STRATA

PREP 20 minutes
BAKE 29 minutes at 450°F
COOK 8 minutes
COOL 5 minutes

1   4-oz. plain bagel, cut into pieces (2⅓ cups)
1   Tbsp. unsalted butter
⅓   cup thinly sliced leek
5   oz. asparagus, trimmed and cut into pieces (1½ cups)
5   eggs
1   cup whole milk
3   oz. feta cheese, crumbled
1   Tbsp. chopped fresh dill
¼   tsp. black pepper
8   oz. thinly sliced smoked salmon (lox-style), chopped
    Crème fraîche, feta cheese, capers, and/or fresh dill

1. Preheat oven to 450°F. Spread bagel pieces on a baking sheet. Bake 7 minutes or until toasted.
2. Meanwhile, in a 10-inch oven-going skillet melt butter over medium-high heat. Add leek; cook 3 minutes or until tender, stirring occasionally. Add asparagus; cook 5 minutes more.
3. In a medium bowl whisk together eggs, milk, feta, dill, and pepper. Add the lox and dried bagel pieces; stir to combine. Pour mixture over leek and asparagus in skillet, stirring gently to combine. Cover with foil. Transfer to oven. Bake, covered, 10 minutes. Uncover. Bake 12 to 14 minutes or until a knife inserted in center comes out clean. Cool 5 minutes. Serve with crème fraîche, feta cheese, additional feta cheese, capers, and/or dill. Makes 6 servings.
PER SERVING *279 cal., 15 g fat (8 g sat. fat), 204 mg chol., 774 mg sodium, 15 g carb., 1 g fiber, 5 g sugars, 20 g pro.*

FENNEL AND ASPARAGUS PIE

PREP 30 minutes
BAKE 12 minutes at 425°F/30 minutes at 375°F
STAND 10 minutes

½   15-oz. pkg. rolled refrigerated unbaked piecrust (1 crust)
1   medium fennel bulb
1   lb. fresh asparagus, trimmed and cut into 1-inch pieces

FENNEL AND ASPARAGUS PIE

½   cup chopped onion
¾   cup fat-free milk
2   Tbsp. all-purpose flour
3   eggs
1   Tbsp. snipped fresh basil or 1 tsp. dried basil, crushed
½   tsp. salt
⅛   tsp. black pepper
1   cup shredded part-skim mozzarella cheese (4 oz.)

1. Preheat oven to 425°F. Let piecrust stand at room temperature according to package directions. Line a 9-inch pie plate with piecrust. Crimp edge as desired. Line unpricked pastry with a double thickness of foil. Bake 8 minutes. Remove foil. Bake 4 to 5 minutes more or until pastry is set and dry. Remove from oven. Reduce oven temperature to 375°F.
2. Meanwhile, trim top of fennel bulb, reserving some feathery leaves for garnish. Trim fennel bulb and thinly slice. In a medium-size covered saucepan, cook fennel, asparagus, and onion in a small amount of boiling water 4 to 6 minutes or just until vegetables are tender. Drain vegetables.
3. In a bowl whisk together milk and flour until smooth. Add eggs, basil, salt, and pepper until combined. Spoon fennel mixture into baked piecrust. Sprinkle with cheese. Slowly pour egg mixture over all.
4. Bake, uncovered, 30 to 35 minutes or until egg mixture is set in center. If necessary to prevent overbrowning, cover edge of pie with foil the last 5 to 10 minutes of baking. Let stand 10 minutes before serving. Top with reserved fennel leaves and, if desired, fresh basil leaves. Makes 6 servings.
PER SERVING *290 cal., 15 g fat (6 g sat. fat), 122 mg chol., 524 mg sodium, 28 g carb., 3 g fiber, 4 g sugars, 12 g pro.*

BAKED EGGS WITH ROASTED VEGETABLES

PREP 25 minutes
ROAST 15 minutes at 425°F
BAKE 10 minutes at 375°F

Nonstick cooking spray
3 cups small broccoli florets (about 1 inch in size)
12 oz. yellow potatoes, such as Yukon Gold, cut into ½- to ¾-inch pieces (about 2 cups)
1 large sweet potato, cut into ½- to ¾-inch pieces (about 1 cup)
1 small red onion, cut into thin wedges
2 Tbsp. olive oil
¼ tsp. salt
6 eggs
2 oz. Manchego cheese, shredded (½ cup)
½ tsp. cracked black pepper

1. Preheat oven to 425°F. Coat a 2-quart rectangular baking dish with cooking spray. In a large bowl toss together the next six ingredients (through salt).
2. Spread vegetables in the prepared baking dish. Roast 10 minutes. Stir; roast 5 minutes more or until vegetables are tender and starting to brown. Remove from oven. Reduce oven temperature to 375°F.
3. Using the back of a spoon, make six depressions in the layer of vegetables. Break an egg into a small dish; pour egg into one of the depressions. Repeat with the remaining 5 eggs. Bake 5 minutes. Sprinkle with cheese. Bake 5 to 10 minutes more or until eggs whites are set and yolks are starting to thicken. Sprinkle with pepper. Makes 6 servings.
Tip To make ahead, spread roasted vegetables in a baking dish; cool. Cover and chill 8 to 24 hours. To serve, let chilled vegetables stand at room temperature 30 minutes. Meanwhile, preheat oven to 375°F. Bake 5 minutes. Continue as directed in Step 3.
PER SERVING *232 cal., 12 g fat (4 g sat. fat), 218 mg chol., 332 mg sodium, 21 g carb., 4 g fiber, 4 g sugars, 11 g pro.*

SPICY BRUNCH LASAGNA

PREP 40 minutes
CHILL 8 hours
STAND 35 minutes
BAKE 1 hour at 350°F

1½ lb. bulk Italian sausage
1 24-oz. carton cottage cheese
½ cup finely chopped green onions
¼ cup snipped fresh chives
¼ cup finely shredded carrot
18 eggs
⅓ cup milk
½ tsp. salt
½ tsp. black pepper
2 Tbsp. butter
1 15- to 16-oz. jar Alfredo sauce
1 tsp. dried Italian seasoning, crushed
8 no-boil lasagna noodles
4 cups frozen shredded hash brown potatoes, thawed
2 cups shredded mozzarella cheese (8 oz.)
Sliced cherry tomatoes (optional)

1. In a large skillet cook sausage until browned. Drain off fat. Meanwhile, in a bowl combine cottage cheese, green onions, chives, and carrot.
2. In an extra-large bowl whisk together eggs, milk, salt, and pepper. In a large skillet melt butter over medium heat. Add egg mixture. Cook, without stirring,

BAKED EGGS WITH ROASTED VEGETABLES

SPICY BRUNCH
LASAGNA

until mixture begins to set on the bottom and around the edges. Using a spatula, lift and fold the partially cooked egg mixture so the uncooked portion flows underneath. Continue cooking 2 to 3 minutes more or until egg mixture is cooked but still glossy and moist. Remove from heat.

3. Stir together Alfredo sauce and Italian seasoning. Spread about ½ cup sauce on the bottom of a 9×13-inch baking dish. Layer half the lasagna noodles over

sauce, overlapping as necessary. Top with half the remaining sauce, half the cottage cheese mixture, half the hash browns, half the scrambled egg mixture, and half the sausage mixture. Sprinkle with half the mozzarella cheese. Repeat layers.

4. Cover baking dish tightly with plastic wrap. Chill 8 to 24 hours.

5. Let lasagna stand at room temperature 30 minutes before baking. Preheat oven to 350°F. Remove plastic wrap; cover baking dish with foil. Bake 45 minutes.

Remove foil. Bake 15 minutes more or until heated through. Let stand 5 minutes before serving. If desired, top with sliced tomatoes and additional chopped green onions. Makes 16 servings.

PER SERVING *452 cal., 30 g fat (12 g sat. fat), 290 mg chol., 918 mg sodium, 19 g carb., 1 g fiber, 2 g sugars, 24 g pro.*

ROASTED VEGETABLES AND CHICKPEAS

PREP 30 minutes
ROAST 45 minutes at 425°F

1   lb. carrots, peeled and cut into
       2-inch pieces
1   lb. sweet potatoes, peeled and cut
       into chunks
1   large red onion, peeled, halved,
       and cut into 1-inch wedges
1   lb. red or russet potatoes, cubed
6   cloves garlic, minced
1   16-oz. can garbanzo beans
       (chickpeas), rinsed and drained
2   to 3 Tbsp. olive oil
1   tsp. dried rosemary, crushed
1   tsp. packed brown sugar
½   tsp. kosher salt
½   tsp. black pepper
       Snipped fresh rosemary (optional)

1. Position an oven rack in center of oven.
Preheat oven to 425°F. Place the first
six ingredients (through chickpeas) in a
9×13-inch pan. In a bowl whisk together
the next five ingredients (through pepper).
Drizzle over vegetables; toss to coat.
2. Roast, uncovered, 45 minutes or until
vegetables are lightly browned and

tender, stirring twice. If desired, sprinkle
with snipped fresh rosemary. Makes
8 servings.
PER SERVING *223 cal., 4 g fat (0 g sat. fat),
0 mg chol., 301 mg sodium, 42 g carb.,
7 g fiber, 9 g sugars, 6 g pro.*

BREAKFAST PIZZA

(PHOTO, PAGE 42)

PREP 15 minutes
BAKE 20 minutes at 375°F
COOK 10 minutes

1   16-oz. loaf frozen whole wheat
       bread dough, thawed
1   cup sliced zucchini, halved, and/or
       green or red sweet pepper pieces
1   cup sliced fresh mushrooms
¼   tsp. crushed red pepper (optional)
1   Tbsp. vegetable oil
8   eggs
½   cup milk
1   Tbsp. butter or margarine
1½   cups shredded cheddar and/or
       mozzarella cheese (6 oz.)
2   slices bacon, crisp-cooked,
       drained, and crumbled
       Bottled salsa (optional)

1. Grease a 13-inch pizza pan. Preheat
oven to 375°F. On a lightly floured surface
roll bread dough into a 14-inch circle. (If
dough is difficult to roll, let it rest a few
minutes.) Transfer dough to prepared
pan. Build up edges slightly. Prick dough
generously with a fork. Bake 15 to
20 minutes or until light brown.
2. Meanwhile, in a large skillet cook
zucchini, mushrooms, and, if desired,
crushed red pepper in hot oil for 5 minutes
or until vegetables are crisp-tender.
Remove zucchini mixture and drain.
3. In a bowl beat together eggs and
milk. In the same skillet melt butter over
medium heat; pour in egg mixture. Cook,
without stirring, until mixture begins to set
on the bottom and around edges. Using
a large spatula, lift and fold partially
cooked eggs so the uncooked portion
flows underneath. Continue cooking over
medium heat for 2 to 3 minutes or until
egg is cooked through but still glossy and
moist. Remove from heat.

4. Sprinkle half the shredded cheese on
the hot crust. Top with scrambled eggs,
zucchini mixture, bacon, and remaining
cheese. Bake 5 to 8 minutes more or until
cheese is melted. If desired, serve with
salsa. Makes 8 servings.
PER SERVING *353 cal., 19 g fat (8 g sat. fat),
241 mg chol., 581 mg sodium, 29 g carb.,
3 g fiber, 0 g sugars, 20 g pro.*

SWEET POTATO-CURRANT LATKES

PREP 25 minutes
COOK 4 minutes

¼   cup dried currants
2   eggs, lightly beaten
⅓   cup finely chopped hazelnuts
¼   tsp. ground cinnamon
¼   tsp. ground cloves
⅛   tsp. salt
1½   lb. sweet potatoes, peeled and
       finely shredded (about 3 cups)
2   Tbsp. vegetable oil

1. In a small bowl pour 1 cup boiling water
over currants; let stand 5 minutes, then
drain. In a large bowl combine eggs,
hazelnuts, drained currants, cinnamon,
cloves, and salt. Stir potatoes into
egg mixture.
2. Using ⅓ cup mixture for each latke,
squeeze batter over a separate small
bowl to remove excess liquid, then shape
into 2½-inch patties. (Discard liquid).
3. In a 12-inch skillet heat oil over medium-
high heat. Place patties in skillet. Cook
4 minutes or until latkes are golden brown,
turning once (if necessary, reduce heat to
medium to prevent overbrowning). Drain
on paper towels. Makes 6 servings.
PER SERVING *164 cal., 8 g fat (1 g sat. fat),
47 mg chol., 101 mg sodium, 21 g carb.,
1 g fiber, 7 g sugars, 4 g pro.*

ROASTED VEGETABLES AND CHICKPEAS

SWEET POTATO-
CURRANT
POTATO LATKES

BLUEBERRY-PEACH CUSTARD KUCHEN

CRANBERRY-BLACK WALNUT COFFEE CAKE

PREP 45 minutes
BAKE 1 hour 15 minutes at 325°F
COOL 15 minutes

2   cups dried cranberries (8 oz.), coarsely chopped
1   cup apple juice or apple cider
1   cup packed brown sugar
2   inches stick cinnamon
3   cups all-purpose flour
½   cup granulated sugar
1   cup black or English walnuts, toasted and ground
2   tsp. baking powder
1   tsp. ground cinnamon
¼   tsp. salt
4   eggs
1   cup milk
1   cup butter, melted
1   tsp. vanilla
1   recipe Walnut Streusel Topping

1. Grease a 10-inch springform pan; set aside. In a medium saucepan combine cranberries, apple juice, ½ cup of the brown sugar, and stick cinnamon. Bring to boiling, stirring to dissolve sugar; reduce heat. Simmer, uncovered, about 15 minutes to reduce liquid. Remove from heat; cool completely. Discard stick cinnamon.
2. Preheat oven to 325°F. In a large bowl stir together the remaining ½ cup brown sugar, the flour, granulated sugar, ground nuts, baking powder, ground cinnamon, and salt. In a medium bowl beat eggs with a fork. Stir in milk, melted butter, and vanilla. Add egg mixture all at once to flour mixture, stirring just until moistened. Spread batter into prepared pan. Sprinkle cranberries over batter to within 1 inch of edge.
3. Sprinkle with Walnut Streusel Topping. Bake 1¼ hours or until edges are lightly browned and begin to pull away from the pan. Cool in pan 15 minutes. Remove sides of pan; serve warm. Makes 12 servings.
Walnut Streusel Topping In a medium bowl stir together ⅔ cup all-purpose flour, ½ cup packed brown sugar, and ¾ teaspoon ground cinnamon. Using a pastry blender, cut in ⅓ cup cold butter, cut up. Stir in ¼ cup chopped black or English walnuts.
PER SERVING 647 cal., 31 g fat (14 g sat. fat), 118 mg chol., 337 mg sodium, 87 g carb., 3 g fiber, 52 g sugars, 10 g pro.

BLUEBERRY-PEACH CUSTARD KUCHEN

PREP 30 minutes
RISE 45 minutes
BAKE 45 minutes at 375°F

2¼   cups all-purpose flour
1   pkg. active dry yeast
½   cup sugar
½   cup milk
¼   cup butter
½   tsp. salt
2   eggs
1   cup peeled and sliced fresh peaches or frozen unsweetened peach slices, thawed
1   cup fresh or thawed, frozen blueberries
1   egg, lightly beaten
2   Tbsp. sugar
½   tsp. vanilla
⅛   tsp. salt
⅛   tsp. ground nutmeg
½   cup half-and-half or light cream
      Ground cinnamon (optional)

1. Grease a 9-inch pie plate; set aside. In a large bowl stir together 1 cup of the flour and the yeast.

2. In a small saucepan heat and stir ½ cup sugar, milk, butter, and ½ teaspoon salt just until warm (120°F to 130°F) and butter is almost melted. Add milk mixture to flour mixture; add 2 eggs. Beat with a mixer on low to medium 30 seconds, scraping sides of bowl constantly. Beat on high 2 minutes or until smooth. Beat in as much of the remaining flour as you can with the mixer. Stir in any remaining flour. (Batter will be stiff.)
3. Spread batter in the prepared pie plate. Top with peach slices and blueberries. Cover and let rise in a warm place until nearly double in size (about 45 minutes).
4. Preheat oven to 375°F. In a medium bowl combine 1 egg, 2 tablespoons sugar, vanilla, ⅛ teaspoon salt, and nutmeg. Stir in half-and-half. Pour mixture over fruit.
5. Place pie plate on a baking sheet; place on oven rack. Bake 45 to 55 minutes or until golden. Cool on a wire rack. If desired, sprinkle servings with cinnamon. Makes 10 servings.
PER SERVING 253 cal., 8 g fat (4 g sat. fat), 73 mg chol., 221 mg sodium, 39 g carb., 2 g fiber, 15 g sugars, 6 g pro.

CRANBERRY-BLACK WALNUT
COFFEE CAKE

PBJ STRUDEL

PBJ STRUDEL

PREP 30 minutes
STAND 10 minutes
COOK 30 minutes
BAKE 20 minutes at 400°F

⅓ cup granulated sugar
1 Tbsp. cornstarch
1½ cups sliced fresh strawberries
⅔ cup peanut butter
¼ cup nonfat dry milk powder
¼ cup powdered sugar
½ 17-oz. pkg. frozen puff pastry
 (1 sheet), thawed according to
 package directions
1 egg
1 Tbsp. water
1 Tbsp. coarse sugar
1 Tbsp. finely chopped peanuts
 (optional)

1. Preheat oven to 400°F. In a small saucepan stir together granulated sugar and cornstarch. Stir in strawberries until sugar is dissolved. Let stand 10 minutes.
2. Meanwhile, in a bowl stir together peanut butter, dry milk, and powdered sugar until well combined.
3. Bring strawberry mixture to boiling over medium heat, stirring until thickened and bubbly. Reduce heat. Cook and stir 2 minutes more. Remove from heat. Cool slightly.
4. On a lightly floured surface unfold and roll out pastry to a 10×14-inch rectangle. Loosely fold into quarters to transfer to a baking sheet lined with parchment paper. Unfold and center on the sheet. With kitchen shears or a sharp knife, cut 3-inch-long strips, 1 inch apart, into the long sides of pastry.
5. Arrange the peanut butter filling along the center of the pastry, pressing into a 3-inch-wide ribbon. Top evenly with strawberry filling. Alternating between sides, crisscross the pastry strips over the filling at a slight angle, overlapping the ends and tucking the last strips underneath. In a small bowl whisk together egg and water; brush over pastry. Sprinkle with coarse sugar and, if desired, peanuts.
6. Bake 20 to 25 minutes or until golden brown. Cool slightly on baking sheet on a wire rack. Serve warm or at room temperature. Makes 8 servings.
PER SERVING *379 cal., 23 g fat (5 g sat. fat), 24 mg chol., 188 mg sodium, 36 g carb., 2 g fiber, 19 g sugars, 9 g pro.*

**BROWN SUGAR-BACON
MONKEY BREAD**

BROWN SUGAR-BACON MONKEY BREAD

PREP 35 minutes
RISE 45 minutes
BAKE 35 minutes at 350°F
COOL 10 minutes

4 slices applewood smoked bacon
1 cup packed brown sugar
⅓ cup Maple-Nut Butter
¼ cup whipping cream
1 Tbsp. vanilla
¼ tsp. Chinese five-spice powder or
 ground allspice
1 16-oz. frozen sweet roll dough,
 thawed
1 cup chopped pecans
1 cup golden raisins

1. In a large skillet cook bacon over medium heat until crisp. Drain, reserving 2 tablespoons drippings in skillet. Drain bacon on paper towels; crumble bacon. Add brown sugar, Maple-Nut Butter, and whipping cream to the skillet; stir until melted. Stir in vanilla and spice.
2. Lightly grease a 10-inch fluted tube pan. Cut thawed bread dough into 1- to 1½-inch pieces. Arrange one-third of the bread pieces, half the crumbled bacon, half the pecans, and half the raisins in the prepared pan. Drizzle one-third of the brown sugar mixture evenly over bread pieces in pan. Top with another one-third of the bread pieces and the remaining bacon, pecans, and raisins. Drizzle with another one-third of the brown sugar mixture. Top with the remaining bread pieces and remaining brown sugar mixture. Cover and let rise in a warm place until nearly double in size (about 45 minutes).
3. Preheat oven to 350°F. Bake 35 to 40 minutes or until bread springs back when lightly touched. Cool in pan on a wire rack 10 minutes. Invert onto a serving platter; remove pan. Serve warm. Makes 10 servings.
Maple-Nut Butter In a food processor combine 1 cup softened butter, ½ cup toasted pecan halves (tip, page 14), and ¼ cup pure maple syrup. Cover and process until nuts are finely chopped. Store leftover nut butter in the refrigerator; serve with pancakes, waffles, or French toast. Makes about 1½ cups.
PER SERVING *430 cal., 20 g fat (7 g sat. fat), 48 mg chol., 170 mg sodium, 60 g carb., 3 g fiber, 37 g sugars, 6 g pro.*

RASPBERRY
ECLAIRS

RASPBERRY ECLAIRS

PREP 1 hour 15 minutes
CHILL 4 hours
BAKE 30 minutes at 400°F

1   recipe Raspberry Filling
1   cup water
½   cup butter
⅛   tsp. salt
1   cup all-purpose flour
4   eggs
     Fresh raspberries (optional)
2   oz. white baking chocolate with
     cocoa butter, coarsely chopped
½   tsp. shortening

1. Prepare Raspberry Filling. Chill as
directed.
2. Preheat oven to 400°F. Line a large
baking sheet with parchment paper; set
aside. In a medium saucepan combine
the water, butter, and salt. Bring to boiling.
Immediately add flour all at once; stir
vigorously. Cook and stir until dough
forms a ball; remove from heat. Cool
10 minutes. Add eggs, one at a time,
beating with a wooden spoon after each
addition until smooth.
3. Spoon dough into a pastry bag fitted
with a large plain round tip (about ½-inch
opening). Slowly pipe 12 strips of dough
3 inches apart onto prepared baking
sheet, making each strip 4 inches long,
1 inch wide, and ¾ inch high.
4. Bake 30 to 35 minutes or until golden
and firm. Transfer to wire racks; cool
completely.

5. To serve, cut eclairs in half lengthwise.
Remove some of the soft dough from
inside. Pipe or spoon Raspberry Filling
into bottom half of each eclair. If desired,
add a few raspberries. Replace top
halves. In a small saucepan heat white
chocolate and shortening over low heat
just until melted and smooth. Drizzle white
chocolate on top. Makes 12 servings.
Raspberry Filling Place 1 cup fresh or
thawed frozen raspberries in a blender
or food processor. Cover and blend or
process until pureed. Strain raspberries
through a fine-mesh sieve (should
have about ½ cup); discard seeds. In
a medium-size heavy saucepan stir
together ¾ cup sugar and 3 tablespoons
cornstarch. Gradually stir in pureed
raspberries, 1 cup heavy cream, and 1 cup
milk. Cook and stir over medium heat
until thickened and bubbly. Cook and
stir 1 minute more. Gradually stir about
half the hot filling into 5 lightly beaten
egg yolks. Return egg yolk mixture to
saucepan. Bring to boiling; reduce
heat. Cook and stir 2 minutes. Pour into
a medium bowl; stir in 2 tablespoons
raspberry liqueur (if desired) and
1 teaspoon vanilla. Tint with red food
coloring to desired color. Place the
bowl of filling in a bowl of ice water; chill
5 minutes, stirring occasionally. Cover
surface with plastic wrap. Chill 4 hours or
until cold.
PER SERVING *323 cal., 21 g fat
(12 g sat. fat), 188 mg chol., 140 mg sodium,
29 g carb., 1 g fiber, 17 g sugars, 6 g pro.*

APPLE-WALNUT DOUGHNUTS

PREP 25 minutes
BAKE 15 minutes at 350°F

     Nonstick cooking spray
1¼   cups white whole wheat flour
½   tsp. baking soda
½   tsp. ground cinnamon
¼   tsp. salt
½   cup plain low-fat yogurt
½   cup packed brown sugar
1   egg, lightly beaten
2   Tbsp. canola oil
2   tsp. vanilla
¾   cup finely chopped unpeeled
     apple
¼   cup finely chopped toasted
     walnuts (tip, page 14)
¼   cup walnuts, toasted and ground
1   tsp. granulated sugar
½   tsp. ground cinnamon
½   cup powdered sugar
1   Tbsp. milk

1. Preheat oven to 350°F. Coat a
standard-size (3½-inch) doughnut
pan* or twelve 2½-inch muffin cups
with cooking spray. In a bowl combine
the next four ingredients (through salt).
In another bowl combine the next five
ingredients (through vanilla); whisk
until smooth. Add yogurt mixture,
apple, and walnuts to flour mixture; stir
until combined.
2. Spoon batter into a large resealable
plastic bag. Using scissors, cut off a
corner; squeeze batter into prepared
pan, filling each cup about two-thirds full.
Smooth tops.
3. Bake 15 minutes or until doughnuts are
almost firm when lightly pressed. Cool
in pan on a wire rack 3 minutes. Transfer
doughnuts to wire rack; cool completely.
4. In a bowl stir together ground walnuts,
sugar, and ½ teaspoon cinnamon. For
icing, in bowl stir together powdered
sugar and milk until smooth. Dip cooled
doughnuts into icing, allowing excess to
drip back into bowl. Transfer to a wire rack
covered with waxed paper. Sprinkle with
walnut mixture. Let stand until icing is set.
Makes 12 servings.
***Tip** If necessary, bake doughnuts in two
batches, washing pan and coating with
cooking spray before filling with batter.
PER SERVING *169 cal., 6 g fat (1 g sat. fat),
16 mg chol., 118 mg sodium, 26 g carb.,
2 g fiber, 16 g sugars, 4 g pro.*

APPLE-WALNUT
DOUGHNUTS

TRIPLE-SPICED
PEAR BREAD

TRIPLE-SPICED PEAR BREAD

PREP 20 minutes
BAKE 50 minutes at 350°F
COOL 10 minutes

3	cups all-purpose flour
2	tsp. baking powder
1	tsp. ground ginger
½	tsp. baking soda
½	tsp. ground cinnamon
½	tsp. salt
¼	tsp. cardamom
1	cup buttermilk
1	cup milk
4	eggs, lightly beaten
½	cup melted butter
½	cup granulated sugar
½	cup packed brown sugar
1	tsp. vanilla
2	cups peeled and chopped pear
¾	cup regular rolled oats, divided
¾	cup toasted walnuts, chopped*

1. Preheat oven to 350°F. Grease the bottom and ½ inch up the sides of two 8×4×2-inch loaf pans. In a large bowl combine the first seven ingredients (through cardamom); make a well in the center.

2. In a medium bowl combine the next seven ingredients (through vanilla). Add to the flour mixture. Stir until just combined. Stir in pear, ½ cup of the oats, and the nuts. Divide batter between prepared pans. Sprinkle with the remaining ¼ cup oats.

3. Bake 50 to 60 minutes or until a toothpick inserted near centers comes out clean. (If necessary to prevent overbrowning, cover bread loosely with foil the last 15 minutes of baking.) Cool in pans on a wire rack 10 minutes. Remove from pans. Cool completely. Makes 28 servings.

*Tip To toast walnuts spread on a sheet pan and bake at 350°F for 5 to 10 minutes or until lightly browned and fragrant. Cool before chopping.

PER SERVING *162 cal., 7 g fat (3 g sat. fat), 37 mg chol., 150 mg sodium, 23 g carb., 1 g fiber, 10 g sugars, 4 g pro.*

CARAMEL-HAZELNUT
CAFE MOCHA

VANILLA BEAN INFUSED HOT CHOCOLATE

SALSA BLOODY MARY

CARAMEL-HAZELNUT CAFE MOCHA

PREP 10 minutes
SLOW COOK 5 hours (low)

8   cups half-and-half or light cream
½   cup chocolate-hazelnut spread
½   cup caramel dessert sauce
¼   cup unsweetened cocoa powder
2   to 3 Tbsp. instant espresso coffee
    powder
    Whipped cream
    Caramel dessert sauce (optional)

1. In a 3½- or 4-quart slow cooker whisk together half-and-half, chocolate-hazelnut spread, the ½ cup caramel sauce, the cocoa powder, and espresso powder.
2. Cover; cook on low 5 to 6 hours, whisking once or twice during cooking if possible, and again before serving.
3. Serve topped with whipped cream and, if desired, drizzle with additional caramel sauce. Makes 12 servings.
Tip If desired, add hazelnut liqueur (Frangelico) to each mug before adding the hot drink.
PER SERVING *347 cal., 25 g fat (15 g sat. fat), 70 mg chol., 111 mg sodium, 26 g carb., 1 g fiber, 22 g sugars, 7 g pro.*

VANILLA BEAN INFUSED HOT CHOCOLATE

PREP 20 minutes
CHILL 2 hours

4   cups whole milk
2   cups heavy cream
2   4- to 6-inch vanilla beans
14   oz. bittersweet chocolate or
     semisweet chocolate, coarsely
     chopped
     Sugar (optional)
     Whipped cream

1. In a large heavy saucepan heat the milk and cream over medium heat until hot, but not boiling. Remove from heat. Using the tip of a paring knife, slit vanilla beans down the center. Using the side of the knife, scrape out seeds. Place seeds and vanilla pods into the hot milk mixture. Cover and chill, allowing vanilla pods to infuse milk with flavor at least 2 hours or overnight.
2. When ready to make hot chocolate, remove vanilla pods and, using two fingers, press milk out of pods to extract all the seeds; discard pods. Heat the milk mixture over medium heat until hot, but not boiling. Add the chocolate. Whisk until the mixture is smooth and chocolate is melted. Add sugar to sweeten, if you like. Top with whipped cream. Makes 15 servings.

PER SERVING *311 cal., 27 g fat (17 g sat. fat), 62 mg chol., 42 mg sodium, 18 g carb., 2 g fiber, 13 g sugars, 4 g pro.*

SALSA BLOODY MARY

START TO FINISH 10 minutes

4   cups vegetable juice
1   16-oz. jar salsa
⅓   cup lime juice
1   Tbsp. prepared horseradish
½   tsp. celery salt
2   cups vodka
     Bottled hot pepper sauce
     (optional)
     Chili powder and kosher salt
     (optional)
     Cucumber spears (optional)
1   avocado, halved, seeded, peeled,
     and sliced (optional)

1. In a blender combine the first five ingredients (through celery salt). Cover and blend to desired consistency. Stir in vodka and, if desired hot pepper sauce. Cover and chill.
2. If desired, coat rims of glasses by pouring a little water on a small plate. On another small plate combine chili powder and kosher salt. Dip rims in water then salt mixture, twisting glass. Serve over ice, if desired with cucumber spears and avocado slices. Makes 8 servings.
PER SERVING *174 cal., 0 g fat, 0 mg chol., 717 mg sodium, 10 g carb., 2 g fiber, 7 g sugars, 2 g pro.*

Home-Baked Breads

At the time of year when you want your home to be as warm and inviting as possible, the aroma of bread baking in the oven is a fragrant solution. This assortment of breads and pastries—both sweet and savory—suits any occasion or time for baking.

GINGERBREAD CINNAMON BUNS, PAGE 63

NO-KNEAD
CHOCOLATE
AND COCONUT
ROLLS

NO-KNEAD CHOCOLATE AND COCONUT ROLLS

PREP 40 minutes
RISE 45 minutes
CHILL 2 hours
STAND 30 minutes
BAKE 15 minutes at 350°F
COOL 5 minutes

4   cups all-purpose flour
1   pkg. active dry yeast
1   cup milk
⅓   cup sugar
¼   cup butter
½   tsp. salt
2   eggs
1   13-oz. jar chocolate-hazelnut spread
1   cup shredded coconut

1. In a large bowl combine 2 cups of the flour and the yeast; set aside. In a small saucepan heat and stir milk, sugar, butter, and salt just until warm (120°F to 130°F) and butter is almost melted. Add milk mixture and eggs to flour mixture. Beat with a mixer on low to medium 30 seconds, scraping sides of bowl constantly. Beat on medium 3 minutes. Stir in the remaining 2 cups flour. Cover; let rise in a warm place until double in size (45 to 60 minutes).
2. Turn dough out onto a well-floured surface. Cover; let rest 10 minutes. Lightly grease a large baking sheet; set aside. Roll dough into a 12×9-inch rectangle. Spread ⅔ cup of the chocolate-hazelnut spread on dough, leaving a 1-inch edge along one long side. (Reserve remaining chocolate-hazelnut spread for icing.) Sprinkle coconut on chocolate-hazelnut spread. Starting from the long side with filling spread to the edge, roll dough into a spiral. Pinch to seal seam. Cut into 8 slices. Arrange slices 2 inches apart on prepared baking sheet. Cover loosely with plastic wrap. (To serve today, let rise in a warm place until nearly double in size [about 45 minutes]. Omit Step 3 and continue as directed in Step 4.)

3. Chill at least 2 hours or up to 24 hours. Let stand at room temperature 30 minutes before baking.
4. Preheat oven to 350°F. Bake 15 to 20 minutes or until golden. Cool 5 minutes; transfer to a wire rack. Drizzle with chocolate-hazelnut icing. Serve warm.
5. For the chocolate hazelnut icing, In a small bowl stir together the remaining chocolate-hazelnut spread and enough milk to make drizzling consistency (2 to 3 tablespoons). Makes 8 servings.
PER SERVING *590 cal., 24 g fat (8 g sat. fat), 64 mg chol., 272 mg sodium, 83 g carb., 3 g fiber, 14 g sugars, 12 g pro.*

GINGERBREAD CINNAMON BUNS

(PHOTO, PAGE 60)

PREP 30 minutes
STAND 5 minutes
RISE 1 hour 45 minutes
BAKE 22 minutes at 350°F
COOL 5 minutes

¼   cup warm water (105°F to 115°F)
2   pkg. active dry yeast
½   cup evaporated milk
⅓   cup mild-flavor or full-flavor molasses
¼   cup packed brown sugar
1   egg, lightly beaten
2   Tbsp. vegetable oil
½   tsp. salt
3¾ to 4 cups all-purpose flour
¼   cup packed brown sugar
2   Tbsp. granulated sugar
1   tsp. ground cinnamon
½   tsp. ground ginger
¼   tsp. ground cloves
2   Tbsp. butter, softened
1   recipe Spiced Glaze
    Cinnamon red hot candies (optional)

1. In a large bowl combine warm water and yeast, stirring to dissolve yeast. Let stand 5 minutes. Stir in evaporated milk, molasses, ¼ cup brown sugar, the egg, oil, and salt. Stir in as much of the flour as you can.

2. Turn dough out onto a lightly floured surface. Knead in enough remaining flour to make a moderately soft dough that is smooth and elastic (3 to 5 minutes total). Shape dough into a ball. Place in a lightly greased bowl, turning once to grease surface. Cover and let rise in a warm place until double in size (1 to 1½ hours).
3. Punch down dough. Turn out onto a lightly floured surface. Cover and let stand 10 minutes. Lightly grease a 9×13-inch baking pan. For filling, combine ¼ cup brown sugar, the granulated sugar, cinnamon, ginger, and cloves.
4. Roll dough into a 12×8-inch rectangle. Spread dough with butter. Sprinkle with filling, leaving 1 inch unfilled along one long side. Roll up rectangle, starting from filled long side. Pinch dough to seal seams. Cut into 12 slices. Arrange rolls in the prepared pan. Cover and let rise in a warm place until nearly double in size (about 45 minutes).
5. Preheat oven to 350°F. Bake 22 to 25 minutes or until golden brown. Cool in pan on a wire rack 5 minutes. Drizzle with Spiced Glaze. If desired, decorate with cinnamon red hot candies. Serve warm. Makes 12 servings.
Spiced Glaze Stir together 1½ cups powdered sugar, 1 tablespoon milk, ½ teaspoon ground cinnamon, and ½ teaspoon vanilla. Stir in additional milk, 1 teaspoon at a time, to make drizzling consistency.
PER SERVING *332 cal., 6 g fat (2 g sat. fat), 26 mg chol., 136 mg sodium, 64 g carb., 1 g fiber, 32 g sugars, 6 g pro.*

PLUM-ALMOND KUCHEN ROLL

PREP 1 hour
RISE 1 hour 30 minutes
REST 10 minutes
BAKE 20 minutes at 375°F
COOL 45 minutes

4½ to 5 cups all-purpose flour
1   pkg. active dry yeast
1   cup milk
½   cup granulated sugar
⅓   cup butter
½   tsp. salt
2   eggs
1   cup packed brown sugar
⅓   cup all-purpose flour
⅓   cup butter
2   cups chopped pitted fresh plums or 1 cup pitted dried plums*
¼   tsp. almond extract
1   recipe Butter Icing
2   Tbsp. sliced almonds, toasted (tip, page 105) (optional)

1. In a large bowl combine 2 cups of the flour and the yeast; set aside. In a small saucepan heat and stir milk, granulated sugar, ⅓ cup butter, and the salt just until warm (120°F to 130°F) and butter is almost melted. Add milk mixture and eggs to flour mixture. Beat with a mixer on low to medium 30 seconds, scraping sides of bowl constantly. Beat on high 3 minutes. Stir in as much of the remaining 2½ to 3 cups flour as you can.

2. Turn dough out onto a floured surface. Knead in enough remaining flour to make a moderately soft dough that is smooth and elastic (3 to 5 minutes total). Shape dough into a ball. Place dough in a lightly greased bowl, turning once to grease surface of dough. Cover and let rise in a warm place until double in size (1 to 1½ hours).

3. Punch dough down. Turn onto a lightly floured surface. Divide in half. Cover with a clean kitchen towel and let rest 10 minutes. Lightly grease a large baking sheet; set aside. For filling, in a medium bowl stir together brown sugar and ⅓ cup flour. Using a pastry blender, cut in ⅓ cup butter until mixture resembles coarse crumbs. Stir in plums and almond extract.

4. Roll each dough half into a 14×8-inch rectangle. Sprinkle filling on dough, leaving 1 inch unfilled along one the long side. Roll up each rectangle, starting from the filled long side. Pinch dough to seal seams and ends. Place rolls on the prepared baking sheet. Cover and let rise in a warm place until nearly double in size (about 30 minutes).

5. Preheat oven to 375°F. Bake 20 to 25 minutes or until golden and bread sounds hollow when lightly tapped. Cool on baking sheet on a wire rack at least 45 minutes. Spread Butter Icing on each loaf. If desired, sprinkle with almonds. Makes 24 servings.

Butter Icing In a small bowl combine 3 tablespoons softened butter and 1 teaspoon vanilla. Gradually stir in 2 cups powdered sugar. Stir in milk (1 to 2 tablespoons), 1 teaspoon at a time, until icing reaches spreading consistency. Makes about ¾ cup.

*Tip If using dried plums, place in a small bowl; cover with boiling water. Let stand 5 minutes. Drain and chop.

PER SERVING *225 cal., 8 g fat (4 g sat. fat), 36 mg chol., 109 mg sodium, 35 g carb., 1 g fiber, 16 g sugars, 4 g pro.*

APPLE PIE PULL-APART LOAF

PREP 30 minutes
STAND 5 minutes
RISE 1 hour 30 minutes
BAKE 45 minutes at 350°F
COOL 30 minutes

¾   cup milk
1   pkg. active dry yeast
1   egg, lightly beaten
¼   cup butter, melted
2   Tbsp. granulated sugar
½   tsp. salt
3   cups all-purpose flour
¼   cup butter, melted
1½   cups finely chopped peeled apples
¾   cup packed brown sugar
2   tsp. apple pie spice
1   recipe Creamy Icing

1. In a small saucepan heat the milk just until warm (105°F to 115°F). In a large bowl combine warm milk and yeast; stir until yeast is dissolved. Let stand 5 minutes.

2. Add egg, the ¼ cup melted butter, granulated sugar, and salt to yeast mixture. Beat with mixer on medium until combined. Add half the flour; beat on low 30 seconds, scraping bowl as needed. Beat 3 minutes on medium. Stir in remaining flour. Shape dough into a ball (dough will not be smooth). Place dough in a greased bowl; turn once to grease surface. Cover and let rise in a warm place until nearly double in size (45 to 60 minutes).

3. Grease a 9×5-inch loaf pan. Turn dough out onto a lightly floured surface. Roll dough into a 20×12-inch rectangle. Brush with ¼ cup melted butter. Sprinkle with apples, brown sugar, and apple pie spice. Cut rectangle in half lengthwise to make two 20×6-inch strips. Cut each strip crosswise into five 6×4-inch strips. Carefully make 2 stacks of 5 strips each. Cut each stack into 4×2-inch pieces. Loosely stagger pieces in pan, cut sides up. Cover and let rise in a warm place until nearly double in size (40 to 45 minutes).

4. Preheat oven to 350°F. Bake about 45 minutes or until golden brown and a thermometer inserted near the center registers 200°F. Cool in pan 10 minutes. Remove from pan to serving plate. Drizzle with Creamy Icing. Cool 20 minutes more. Makes 10 servings.

Creamy Icing In a bowl beat together 2 ounces softened cream cheese, 1 cup powdered sugar, and ½ teaspoon vanilla with a mixer on medium until smooth. Beat in enough milk (1 to 2 tablespoons) to make drizzling consistency.

To Make Ahead Prepare as directed through Step 2, except do not let dough rise. Cover bowl and refrigerate up to 24 hours. Let dough stand at room temperature 30 minutes before continuing with Step 3.

PER SERVING *386 cal., 13 g fat (7 g sat. fat), 51 mg chol., 233 mg sodium, 63 g carb., 2 g fiber, 33 g sugars, 6 g pro.*

APPLE PIE
PULL-APART LOAF

ORANGE AND
CHOCOLATE
CHALLAH

ORANGE AND CHOCOLATE CHALLAH

PREP 45 minutes
RISE 2 hours
BAKE 35 minutes at 325°F
STAND 10 minutes
COOL 10 minutes

2¾ to 3¼ cups all-purpose flour
1   pkg. active dry yeast
¾   cup low-fat milk
½   cup sugar
¼   cup butter
½   tsp. salt
1   egg
½   cup chopped pecans, toasted*
¼   cup chopped pitted dates
2   Tbsp. unsweetened cocoa powder
1   Tbsp. orange zest
1   Tbsp. orange liqueur or orange juice
     Milk
1   recipe Two Glazes

1. In a large mixing bowl stir together 1½ cups of the flour and the yeast. In a medium saucepan heat and stir ¾ cup milk, the sugar, butter, and salt just until warm (120°F to 130°F) and butter is almost melted; add to flour mixture along with egg. Beat with a mixer on low 30 seconds, scraping sides of bowl constantly. Beat on high 3 minutes. Stir in ½ cup flour, the pecans, and dates.

2. Place one-third of the dough in a small bowl. Stir in cocoa powder and as much of the remaining flour as needed to get the dough to pull away from the sides of the bowl. Turn dough out onto a lightly floured surface. Knead in enough remaining flour to form a moderately soft dough that is smooth and elastic (3 to 5 minutes). Shape dough into a ball. Place dough in a greased bowl; turn once to grease surface of dough. Cover and set aside.

3. Stir orange zest and orange liqueur into the remaining dough. Stir in as much remaining flour as you can. Turn out orange dough onto a lightly floured surface. Knead in enough remaining flour to make a moderately soft dough that is smooth and elastic (3 to 5 minutes). Shape dough into a ball. Place dough

in a greased bowl; turn once to grease surface of dough. Cover and let doughs rise in a warm place until double (about 1 to 1½ hours).

4. Punch down each dough. Turn out each dough onto a lightly floured surface. Divide orange dough in half. Cover; let rest 10 minutes. Meanwhile, lightly grease a large baking sheet.

5. Shape each portion of dough into a 16-inch-long rope (3 ropes total). Line up ropes about 1 inch apart on prepared baking sheet with the chocolate rope in the center.

6. Starting in the center of the ropes, loosely braid by bringing the left rope under the center rope. Next bring right rope under the new center rope. Repeat to the end. On the other end, braid by bringing alternate ropes over center rope from center to end. Press ends together to seal; tuck under. Cover; let rise in a warm place until nearly double (about 1 hour).

7. Preheat oven to 325°F. Brush loaf with additional milk. Bake 35 minutes or until bread sounds hollow when lightly tapped. If necessary to prevent overbrowning, cover loosely with foil during the last 10 to 15 minutes of baking. Immediately remove from baking sheet. Cool 10 minutes on a wire rack. Drizzle with Two Glazes. Makes 16 servings.

Two Glazes In a medium bowl stir together ¾ cup powdered sugar and 2 teaspoons softened butter. Add enough warm water (2 to 3 teaspoons) to make icing drizzling consistency. Divide icing in half. Stir ½ teaspoon unsweetened cocoa powder into one half; add more warm water, a drop at a time, if necessary, until icing is drizzling consistency. Stir ½ teaspoon orange zest into the other half; add more warm water, a drop at a time, if necessary, until icing is drizzling consistency.

***Tip** To toast large pieces of nuts or coconut, spread in a shallow baking pan. Bake in a 350°F oven 5 to 10 minutes or until golden, stirring pan once or twice and watching closely to prevent burning.

PER SERVING *202 cal., 6 g fat (2 g sat. fat), 22 mg chol., 107 mg sodium, 32 g carb., 1 g fiber, 14 g sugars, 4 g pro.*

LEMON BRIOCHE

LEMON BRIOCHE

PREP 40 minutes
STAND 10 minutes
RISE 1 hour 45 minutes
CHILL 12 hours
BAKE 13 minutes at 375°F
COOL 5 minutes

2   pkg. active dry yeast
⅓   cup warm water (105°F to 115°F)
⅓   cup warm milk (105°F to 115°F)
4   cups all-purpose flour
1½   tsp. salt
4   eggs, room temperature
¼   cup sugar
2   Tbsp. lemon zest
1   cup (2 sticks) butter, room
     temperature

1. In a stand mixer fit with a dough hook dissolve yeast in water and milk. Let stand 10 minutes until yeast is softened. Add flour and salt. Mix on medium-low 2 minutes or until flour is moistened.
2. Reduce speed to low. Separate 1 egg. Add yolk and the remaining 3 eggs (refrigerate egg white for later). Add sugar and lemon zest. Increase speed to medium; beat 3 minutes. Reduce speed to low. Add butter 2 tablespoons at a time, beating until each addition is incorporated before adding the next. Increase speed to medium-high. Continue to beat 10 minutes or until dough pulls away from sides of bowl. Transfer to a greased bowl. Cover; let rise in a warm place until double in size (about 1 hour). Using a spatula, release dough from sides of bowl to deflate slightly. Cover with plastic wrap. Chill 12 to 24 hours.
3. Grease eighteen 3- to 4-inch fluted individual brioche molds or large muffin cups. Pat the cold dough into a 12×6-inch rectangle. Using a dough scraper or sharp knife, cut into 18 equal portions. From each remove a small piece; roll into eighteen 1-inch balls. Roll remaining portions into eighteen larger balls; place in prepared pans. Using your fingers, make a deep indentation in the center of dough ball. Brush with water. Press small balls into indentations. Cover; let rise in a warm place until double in size (about 45 minutes).

4. Preheat oven to 375°F. In a small bowl combine reserved egg white and 1 tablespoon water; brush over dough. Bake 13 to 15 minutes or until golden brown. Cool 5 minutes. Remove from pans. Cool on wire racks. Makes 18 servings.
Loaves Divide dough into 18 portions as above. Roll pieces into balls, placing 9 each in two greased 9×5-inch loaf pans. Increase baking time to 18 to 20 minutes.
PER SERVING *223 cal., 12 g fat (7 g sat. fat), 69 mg chol., 294 mg sodium, 25 g carb., 1 g fiber, 3 g sugars, 5 g pro.*

BEST POTATO ROLLS

PREP 40 minutes
RISE 1 hour 15 minutes
STAND 10 minutes
BAKE 15 minutes at 375°F

2   small russet (baking) potatoes
     (12 oz. total), peeled and cut into
     chunks
1   cup buttermilk
¼   cup butter
2   Tbsp. sugar
2   tsp. salt
5   to 5¾ cups bread flour or
     all-purpose flour
2   pkg. active dry yeast
2   Tbsp. butter, melted

1. In a small saucepan cook potatoes, covered, in enough boiling water to cover 15 to 20 minutes or until tender; drain, reserving ½ cup of the cooking water. Using a fork, mash the potatoes; set aside. Add buttermilk, the ¼ cup butter, sugar, and salt to the hot cooking water; heat until warm (120°F to 130°F) and butter is almost melted.
2. In a large bowl stir together 1½ cups of the flour and the yeast. Stir in the buttermilk mixture and mashed potatoes. Beat with a mixer on low 30 seconds, scraping bowl. Beat on high 3 minutes. Stir in as much remaining flour as you can.

3. Turn dough out onto a lightly floured surface. Knead in enough remaining flour to make a moderately stiff dough that is smooth and elastic (6 to 8 minutes total). Shape dough into a ball. Place in a buttered bowl; turn once. Cover; let rise in a warm place until double (about 1 hour).
4. Punch dough down. Turn dough out onto a lightly floured surface. Divide dough in half. Cover; let rest 10 minutes. Meanwhile, lightly grease three baking sheets (or line baking sheets with parchment paper).
5. Preheat oven to 375°F. On a lightly floured surface, roll each portion of dough into a 10×6-inch rectangle (¾ inch thick). Cut each rectangle of dough into fifteen 2-inch squares. Place squares 2 to 3 inches apart on the prepared baking sheets. Brush tops with the 2 tablespoons melted butter. Cover with plastic wrap; let rise in a warm place 15 minutes.
6. Bake 15 to 18 minutes or until golden. Immediately remove rolls from baking sheet. Cool slightly on a rack. Serve warm. Makes 30 rolls.
PER SERVING *118 cal., 3 g fat (2 g sat. fat), 7 mg chol., 190 mg sodium, 19 g carb., 1 g fiber, 0 g sugars, 3 g pro.*
Garlic and Rosemary Knots Prepare as above. Cut each rectangle of dough into fifteen 6×¾-inch strips. Gently pull strips into 8-inch ropes. In a small bowl combine ¾ cup olive oil, 3 tablespoons snipped fresh rosemary, and 2 cloves garlic, minced. Dip each rope into oil mixture. Tie into a loose knot. Place knots 2 to 3 inches apart on the prepared baking sheets. Sprinkle with coarse or kosher salt. Cover with plastic wrap; let rise in a warm place 15 minutes. Bake 15 minutes or until golden. Immediately remove rolls from baking sheet. Cool slightly on a rack. Serve warm. Makes 30 knots.

SWEET POTATO DINNER BISCUITS

PREP 25 minutes
BAKE 12 minutes at 425°F

2½ cups all-purpose flour
1   Tbsp. baking powder
1½ tsp. salt
⅓   cup shortening, chilled
1   cup mashed sweet potato*
¾   cup milk

1. Preheat oven to 425°F. In a large bowl stir together flour, baking powder, and salt. Use a pastry blender to cut in shortening until mixture resembles coarse crumbs.

2. In a bowl combine mashed sweet potato and milk. Use a fork to gradually stir sweet potato mixture into flour mixture. Do not overmix.

3. Turn dough out onto a floured surface. Knead dough by folding and gently pressing just until dough holds together. Roll or pat dough into an 8×6-inch rectangle. Cut with a floured 2-inch round cutter or use a knife to cut 2-inch squares; reroll scraps as needed and dip cutter into flour between cuts.

4. Place 1 inch apart on an ungreased baking sheet. Bake 12 to 14 minutes or until golden. Serve warm. Makes 12 servings.
*Tip For mashed sweet potato(es), prick one 12-oz. sweet potato in several places with a fork. Microwave 6 to 7 minutes or until very tender. When cool enough to handle, scrape flesh from potato. (Or drain one 15-ounce can sweet potatoes.) Mash sweet potato and measure 1 cup.
PER SERVING *174 cal., 6 g fat (2 g sat. fat), 1 mg chol., 428 mg sodium, 26 g carb., 1 g fiber, 2 g sugars, 4 g pro.*

SPICED NUTS AND ZUCCHINI CORN BREAD

PREP 25 minutes
BAKE 50 minutes at 300°F

1   cup all-purpose flour
1   cup yellow cornmeal
½   cup salt and pepper mixed nuts, finely chopped
⅓   cup sugar
4   tsp. baking powder
¼   tsp. salt
4   eggs
½   cup butter, melted
½   cup unsweetened applesauce
1   14.75-oz. can cream-style corn
1   cup coarsely shredded zucchini
1   cup shredded sharp cheddar cheese (4 oz.)
½   cup finely chopped onion

1. Preheat oven to 300°F. Grease a 9×13-inch baking pan; set aside. In a large bowl stir together the first six ingredients (through salt).

2. In a bowl whisk together the eggs, butter, and applesauce. Stir in the corn, zucchini, cheese, and onion. Add egg mixture all at once to cornmeal mixture. Stir just until moistened. Pour batter into prepared pan.

3. Bake 50 to 60 minutes, just until edges are golden brown. Cool slightly; serve warm. Makes 18 servings.
PER SERVING *201 cal., 11 g fat (5 g sat. fat), 67 mg chol., 326 mg sodium, 21 g carb., 1 g fiber, 6 g sugars, 5 g pro.*

SWEET POTATO DINNER BISCUITS

SPICED NUTS
AND
ZUCCHINI
CORN BREAD

CHOCOLATE-
CHERRY
BANANA BREAD

CHOCOLATE-CHERRY BANANA BREAD

PREP 30 minutes
BAKE 40 minutes at 350°F
COOL 30 minutes
STAND overnight

½ cup snipped dried cherries
¼ cup amaretto, brandy, or orange juice
1½ cups all-purpose flour
⅓ cup unsweetened cocoa powder
1½ tsp. baking powder
1 tsp. ground cinnamon
½ tsp. baking soda
¼ tsp. salt
2 eggs, lightly beaten
1½ cups mashed ripe bananas (4 to 5 medium)
1 cup sugar
½ cup vegetable oil or melted butter
¼ cup pecans, toasted and chopped

1. Grease bottom and ½ inch up the sides of two 7½×3½×2-inch loaf pans; set aside. In a small saucepan combine cherries and amaretto. Heat over low heat just until mixture comes to a simmer (do not boil). Remove from heat; cool to room temperature.

2. Preheat oven to 350°F. In a large bowl combine flour, cocoa, baking powder, cinnamon, baking soda, and salt. Make a well in the center of flour mixture.

3. In a medium bowl combine eggs, bananas, sugar, and oil. Add egg mixture all at once to flour mixture. Stir just until moistened (batter should be lumpy). Fold in soaked cherries and pecans.

4. Spoon batter into prepared pans; spread evenly. Bake 40 to 45 minutes or until a toothpick inserted near center comes out clean. If necessary to prevent overbrowning, cover loosely with foil the last 15 minutes of baking.

5. Cool in pans on a wire rack 10 minutes. Remove from pans. Cool completely on rack. Wrap and store overnight before slicing. Makes 20 servings.

PER SERVING *173 cal., 7 g fat (1 g sat. fat), 19 mg chol., 106 mg sodium, 26 g carb., 1 g fiber, 15 g sugars, 2 g pro.*

HONEY-GLAZED PUMPKIN-BANANA BREAD

PREP 25 minutes
BAKE 50 minutes at 350°F
COOL 10 minutes
STAND overnight

3⅓ cups all-purpose flour
2 tsp. baking soda
1½ tsp. salt
1 tsp. baking powder
1 tsp. ground cinnamon
1 tsp. ground ginger
2 cups sugar
⅔ cup vegetable oil
4 eggs
⅔ cup water
1 15-oz. can pumpkin
½ cup mashed ripe banana
1 recipe Honey Glaze
2 Tbsp. finely chopped crystallized ginger

1. Preheat oven to 350°F. Grease bottom and ½ inch up sides of two 9×5-inch loaf pans; set aside. In a bowl combine the first six ingredients (through ginger).

2. In an extra-large bowl beat sugar and oil with a mixer on medium until combined. Add eggs, one at a time, beating after each addition. Alternately add flour mixture and the water, beating on low after each addition just until combined. Beat in pumpkin and banana. Spoon into prepared pans.

3. Bake 50 to 60 minutes or until a toothpick in centers comes out clean. Cool loaves in pans 10 minutes. Remove from pans; cool on wire racks. Wrap loaves and store overnight before serving. To serve, spoon Honey Glaze over bread. Sprinkle with crystallized ginger. Makes 32 servings.

Honey Glaze In a small bowl beat 2 tablespoons softened butter and ¼ cup honey on medium until combined. Beat in 1 cup powdered sugar. Beat in 1 teaspoon milk for thick drizzling consistency.

PER SERVING *184 cal., 6 g fat (1 g sat. fat), 25 mg chol., 219 mg sodium, 31 g carb., 1 g fiber, 19 g sugars, 2 g pro.*

HONEY-GLAZED PUMPKIN-BANANA BREAD

ORANGE-CHOCOLATE CHIP MUFFINS

ORANGE-CHOCOLATE CHIP MUFFINS

PREP 20 minutes
BAKE 18 minutes at 400°F
COOL 5 minutes

2   oranges
2   cups all-purpose flour
1   Tbsp. baking powder
½   tsp. salt
½   cup miniature semisweet chocolate pieces
2   eggs
½   cup sugar
½   cup milk
¼   cup vegetable oil
1   recipe Streusel Topping

1. Preheat oven to 400°F. Line twelve 2½-inch muffin cups with paper bake cups; set aside. Remove 1 tablespoon zest and ½ cup juice from oranges.
2. In a large bowl stir together flour, baking powder, and salt. Stir in chocolate pieces. Make a well in the center of flour mixture; set aside.
3. In a medium bowl stir together eggs, sugar, milk, orange zest and juice, and oil. Add egg mixture all at once to flour mixture. Stir just until moistened (batter should be lumpy).
4. Spoon ¼ cup of the batter into each prepared muffin cup. Sprinkle generously with Streusel Topping. Bake 18 to 20 minutes or until a wooden toothpick inserted in centers comes out clean.
5. Cool in muffin cups on a wire rack 5 minutes. Remove from muffin cups; serve warm. Makes 12 servings.
Streusel Topping In a medium bowl stir together ½ cup all-purpose flour and ½ cup sugar. Using a pastry blender, cut in ⅓ cup butter by repeatedly pushing down through the butter until the mixture resembles coarse crumbs (rotate pastry blender and bowl to cut in uniformly). Stir in ½ cup chopped walnuts and ¼ cup miniature semisweet chocolate pieces.
PER SERVING *372 cal., 18 g fat (7 g sat. fat), 46 mg chol., 250 mg sodium, 49 g carb., 2 g fiber, 26 g sugars, 6 g pro.*

LEMON CURD
MUFFINS

LEMON CURD MUFFINS

PREP 25 minutes
BAKE 18 minutes at 400°F
COOL 5 minutes

1½ cups all-purpose flour
½ cup granulated sugar
¼ cup whole wheat flour
2 tsp. baking powder
¼ tsp. salt
1 egg
¾ cup milk
¼ cup cooking oil
⅔ cup purchased lemon curd
2 Tbsp. toasted coconut (tip, page 67)

1. Preheat oven to 400°F. Grease six popover pans and line with tall (tulip) paper bake cups; set aside. In a medium bowl stir together the first five ingredients (through salt). Make a well in the center of the dry ingredients; set aside.
2. In a small bowl combine egg, milk, and oil. Add egg mixture all at once to dry ingredients. Stir just until moistened (batter should be lumpy).
3. Spoon half the batter into prepared popover pans (2 rounded tablespoons in each popover pan). Spoon 2 rounded teaspoons of the lemon curd on the batter in each pan. (There will be remaining lemon curd for topping). Spoon remaining batter into popover pans, filling each pan two-thirds full.
4. Bake 18 to 20 minutes or until golden brown. Cool in popover pans on a wire rack 5 minutes. Remove from pans. Top with remaining lemon curd and toasted coconut. Serve warm or cool. Makes 6 servings.
PER SERVING *419 cal., 13 g fat (4 g sat. fat), 65 mg chol., 291 mg sodium, 47 g carb., 5 g fiber, 42 g sugars, 6 g pro.*

BACON-CHEDDAR SCONES

PREP 15 minutes
BAKE 15 minutes at 400°F

1¾ cups all-purpose flour
2 Tbsp. sugar
1 Tbsp. baking powder
¼ tsp. salt
1 cup heavy cream
½ cup shredded cheddar cheese (2 oz.)
4 slices packaged ready-to-serve cooked bacon, chopped
1 egg, lightly beaten
1 Tbsp. water
½ tsp. dried thyme, crushed

1. Preheat oven to 400°F. In a medium bowl stir together flour, sugar, baking powder, and salt. Make a well in center of flour mixture; set aside. In another medium bowl combine cream, cheese, and bacon. Add cream mixture all at once to flour mixture. Using a fork, stir just until moistened.
2. Turn dough out onto a floured surface. Knead dough by folding and gently pressing 10 to 12 strokes or until nearly smooth. Pat or lightly roll into an 8-inch circle. Cut into eight wedges. Place 1 inch apart on an ungreased baking sheet.
3. In a small bowl combine egg and the water. Brush tops of wedges with egg mixture and sprinkle with thyme. Bake 15 minutes or until golden brown. Remove scones from baking sheet. Serve warm. Makes 8 servings.
PER SERVING *265 cal., 15 g fat (9 g sat. fat), 77 mg chol., 318 mg sodium, 25 g carb., 1 g fiber, 3 g sugars, 7 g pro.*

SALTED PECAN AND ORANGE SCONES

PREP 20 minutes
BAKE 13 minutes at 400°F

1	orange
2½	cups all-purpose flour
2	Tbsp. packed brown sugar
1	Tbsp. baking powder
¼	tsp. salt
6	Tbsp. butter
1	egg, lightly beaten
¾	cup heavy cream
1	cup salted pecan halves, toasted (tip, page 105)
½	cup powdered sugar
	Orange peel strips (optional)

1. Remove 2¼ teaspoons zest and 1 tablespoon juice from orange.
2. Preheat oven to 400°F. In a large bowl combine the flour, sugar, baking powder, and salt. Using a pastry blender, cut in butter until mixture resembles coarse crumbs. Make a well in the center of flour mixture.
3. In a medium bowl combine egg, cream, and 2 teaspoons of the orange zest. Add egg mixture all at once to flour mixture. Add pecans. Using a fork, stir just until moistened.
4. Turn dough out onto a lightly floured surface. Knead by folding and gently pressing 10 to 12 strokes or until dough is nearly smooth. Pat into a 10×4-inch rectangle. Cut in half lengthwise and in sixths crosswise to make 12 rectangles.
5. Place rectangles 2 inches apart on a parchment paper-lined baking sheet. Brush wedges with additional cream. Bake 13 to 15 minutes or until golden brown. Remove scones from baking sheet. Cool slightly. Drizzle or brush with orange glaze. If desired, sprinkle with orange peel strips. Serve warm.
6. Meanwhile, for the orange glaze, in a bowl stir together powdered sugar, remaining orange zest, and the orange juice. Makes 12 servings.
PER SERVING *309 cal., 20 g fat (8 g sat. fat), 55 mg chol., 266 mg sodium, 29 g carb., 2 g fiber, 8 g sugars, 5 g pro.*

SALTED PECAN AND ORANGE SCONES

CRANBERRY-WHITE CHOCOLATE SCONES

PREP 20 minutes
BAKE 12 minutes at 400°F

2½	cups all-purpose flour
2	Tbsp. granulated sugar
1	Tbsp. baking powder
½	tsp. salt
⅓	cup butter
2	eggs, lightly beaten
¾	cup heavy cream
¼	cup chopped dried cranberries
¼	cup finely chopped white chocolate (with cocoa butter) or miniature semisweet chocolate pieces
½	tsp. orange zest (optional)
	Heavy cream or milk
1	recipe Orange Drizzle

1. Preheat oven to 400°F. In a large bowl combine flour, granulated sugar, baking powder, and salt. Using a pastry blender, cut in butter until mixture resembles coarse crumbs. Make a well in the center of the flour mixture; set aside.
2. In a medium bowl combine eggs, the ¾ cup cream, cranberries, chopped white chocolate, and, if desired, orange zest. Add egg mixture all at once to flour mixture. Using a fork, stir just until moistened.
3. Turn dough out onto a lightly floured surface. Knead dough by folding and gently pressing 10 to 12 strokes or just until dough comes together. Divide dough in half. Pat or lightly roll each half into a 6-inch circle. Cut each circle into six wedges.
4. Place wedges 2 inches apart on an ungreased baking sheet. Brush wedges with additional cream. Bake 12 to 14 minutes or until golden brown. Cool slightly on baking sheet. Drizzle with Orange Drizzle. Serve warm or at room temperature. Makes 12 servings.
Orange Drizzle In a bowl combine 1 cup powdered sugar, 1 tablespoon orange juice, and ¼ teaspoon vanilla. Stir in additional orange juice, 1 teaspoon at a time, to make drizzling consistency.
PER SERVING *288 cal., 14 g fat (8 g sat. fat), 69 mg chol., 286 mg sodium, 37 g carb., 1 g fiber, 16 g sugars, 4 g pro.*

CRANBERRY-WHITE
CHOCOLATE SCONES

BANANAS FOSTER
CRÈMES BRÛLÉES,
PAGE 86

Sweet Indulgence

Some of the best holiday traditions come out of the oven. Luxurious desserts are one of the sweetest pleasures of the season. Whether decadent cheesecake, fanciful cupcake, or fruity treat, you'll find the finale for your celebration here.

BERRY-WALNUT UPSIDE-DOWN CAKE

PREP 25 minutes
STAND 5 minutes
BAKE 30 minutes at 350°F
COOL 35 minutes

⅔ cup dried tart cherries or dried cranberries
Boiling water
¼ cup butter

½ cup packed brown sugar
2 Tbsp. orange juice
½ cup chopped walnuts, toasted (tip, page 105)
1⅓ cups all-purpose flour
⅔ cup granulated sugar
2 tsp. baking powder
¼ tsp. salt
¼ tsp. ground ginger
⅔ cup milk
¼ cup butter, softened
1 egg

1 tsp. vanilla
Whipped cream (optional)

1. Preheat oven to 350°F. Place cherries in a medium bowl; add enough boiling water to cover. Let stand 5 minutes; drain. Wipe out the bowl; set aside.
2. Meanwhile, place ¼ cup butter in a 9-inch round cake pan. Place cake pan in the oven until butter is melted. Stir brown sugar and orange juice into melted butter.

BERRY-WALNUT UPSIDE-DOWN CAKE

Arrange cherries and walnuts evenly in pan; set aside.

3. In the same medium bowl stir together flour, granulated sugar, baking powder, salt, and ginger. Add milk, ¼ cup softened butter, the egg, and vanilla; beat with a spoon until combined. Beat vigorously 1 minute more. (Batter may still be lumpy.) Spread batter in prepared pan.

4. Bake 30 to 35 minutes or until a toothpick inserted near the center comes out clean. Cool in pan on a wire rack 5 minutes. Loosen sides of cake; invert onto a serving plate. Cool 30 minutes. Serve warm. If desired, top with whipped cream. Makes 8 servings.

PER SERVING *380 cal., 18 g fat (8 g sat. fat), 59 mg chol., 236 mg sodium, 53 g carb., 1 g fiber, 36 g sugars, 4 g pro.*

CREAM-FILLED CAKE ROLL

PREP 30 minutes
STAND 30 minutes
BAKE 12 minutes at 375°F
COOL 1 hour

4	eggs
½	cup all-purpose flour
1	tsp. baking powder
½	tsp. vanilla
⅓	cup granulated sugar
½	cup granulated sugar
	Powdered sugar
1	recipe Lemon-Cream Filling
	Lemon zest

1. Separate eggs. Allow egg whites and yolks to stand at room temperature for 30 minutes. Meanwhile, grease a 15×10×1-inch baking pan. Line bottom of pan with waxed paper or parchment paper; grease paper. Set pan aside. In a medium bowl stir together flour and baking powder.

2. Preheat oven to 375°F. In a medium mixing bowl beat egg yolks and vanilla with a mixer on high 5 minutes or until thick and lemon color. Gradually add ⅓ cup granulated sugar; beat on high until sugar is almost dissolved.

3. Thoroughly wash beaters. In a large bowl beat egg whites with a mixer on medium until soft peaks form (tips curl). Gradually add ½ cup granulated sugar, beating until stiff peaks form (tips stand straight). Fold egg yolk mixture into beaten egg whites. Sprinkle flour mixture over egg mixture; fold in gently just until

CREAM-FILLED CAKE ROLL

combined. Spread batter evenly in the prepared baking pan.

4. Bake 12 to 15 minutes or until cake springs back when lightly touched. Immediately loosen edges of cake from pan and turn out cake onto a clean kitchen towel sprinkled with powdered sugar. Remove waxed paper. Roll towel and cake into a spiral, starting from a narrow side of the cake. Cool for 1 hour on a wire rack. Meanwhile, prepare filling.

5. Unroll cake; remove towel. Spread cake with Lemon-Cream Filling to within 1 inch of edges. Roll up cake; trim ends. Cover and chill up to 6 hours. If desired, top each serving with lemon zest and sprinkle

lightly with additional powdered sugar. Makes 10 servings.

Lemon-Cream Filling In a medium bowl beat one 3-ounce. package softened cream cheese with a mixer on medium until smooth. Beat in ¼ cup lemon curd until combined. In a small bowl beat ½ cup heavy cream on medium until soft peaks form (tips curl); fold into cream cheese mixture.

PER SERVING *219 cal., 10 g fat (5 g sat. fat), 116 mg chol., 90 mg sodium, 30 g carb., 1 g fiber, 24 g sugars, 4 g pro.*

OLIVE OIL CAKE WITH ROASTED CITRUS

PREP 35 minutes
ROAST 10 minutes at 450°F
BAKE 30 minutes at 375°F
COOL 15 minutes

1   recipe Roasted Citrus
2   tsp. butter, softened
2   lemons
½   cup sugar
½   cup slivered almonds, toasted (tip page 105)
2   cups all-purpose flour
1   Tbsp. baking powder
2   tsp. snipped fresh rosemary
½   tsp. salt
3   eggs, lightly beaten
1   cup buttermilk
¼   cup olive oil
½   cup sugar
½   cup water
4   1-inch strips orange zest

1. Prepare Roasted Citrus. Reduce oven temperature to 375°F. Grease a 9×2-inch round cake pan with butter. Remove 1 tablespoon zest and squeeze 3 tablespoons juice from lemons.
2. In a food processor cover and pulse ½ cup sugar and almonds until nuts are finely ground. Transfer to a large bowl. Stir in lemon zest, flour, baking powder, rosemary, and salt. Make a well in center of flour mixture.
3. In a medium bowl combine eggs, buttermilk, oil, and lemon juice. Add all at once to flour mixture, stirring just until combined. Spread batter in prepared pan. Bake 30 minutes or until a toothpick comes out clean. Cool in pan on a wire rack 15 minutes. Remove cake from pan.
4. Meanwhile, for syrup, in a small saucepan combine remaining ingredients. Bring to boiling over medium heat, stirring until sugar is dissolved. Cool and strain; discard zest.
5. Spoon syrup over cake. Top with roasted citrus slices. Serve warm or at room temperature. Makes 10 servings.
Roasted Citrus Preheat oven to 450°F. Line a 15×10-inch baking pan with foil; generously coat foil with nonstick cooking spray. Cut peels from 4 to 5 citrus fruits, such as grapefruits, blood or navel oranges, tangerines, and/or Meyer lemons. Using a serrated knife, cut fruits into ¼-inch slices; place in prepared pan. Sprinkle lightly with sugar. Roast 10 to 15 minutes or until bottoms start to brown. Immediately remove from pan.
PER SERVING *324 cal., 11 g fat (2 g sat. fat), 59 mg chol., 316 mg sodium, 51 g carb., 3 g fiber, 29 g sugars, 7 g pro.*

CRANBERRY LAYER CAKE

PREP 25 minutes
BAKE 25 minutes at 350°F
COOL 10 minutes

2   cups fresh or frozen cranberries
1   pkg. white cake mix (2-layer-size)
1   cup water
⅓   cup vegetable oil
3   eggs
1¼   cups chopped pecans, toasted (tip page 105)
1   Tbsp. orange zest
1   8-oz. pkg. cream cheese, softened
½   cup butter, softened
1   tsp. vanilla
4¾ to 5½ cups powdered sugar
½   tsp. orange zest

1. Preheat oven to 350°F. Rinse cranberries in cold water; drain. Coarsely chop cranberries; set aside. Grease and flour two 8×1½-inch or two 9×1½-inch round cake pans.
2. In a large bowl combine cake mix, the water, oil, and eggs. Beat with a mixer on low just until combined. Beat on medium 2 minutes. Fold in cranberries, 1 cup of the pecans, and the 1 tablespoon orange zest. Divide between prepared pans, spreading evenly.
3. Bake 25 to 30 minutes for 9-inch layer or 30 to 35 minutes for 8-inch layer or until a wooden toothpick inserted near centers comes out clean. Cool cake layers in pans on wire racks for 10 minutes. Remove cake layers from pans. Cool completely on wire racks.
4. For frosting, in a large bowl beat cream cheese, butter, and vanilla with a mixer on medium until light and fluffy. Gradually beat in enough powdered sugar to reach spreading consistency. Stir in ½ teaspoon orange zest.
5. Place one layer on a serving plate. Spread with some of the frosting. Top with second layer. Spread top and sides of cake with remaining frosting. Sprinkle with the remaining ¼ cup pecans. Serve immediately or cover loosely and store in the refrigerator. Let chilled cake stand at room temperature 30 minutes before serving. Serve with glasses of sparkling juice if desired. Makes 12 servings.
PER SERVING *657 cal., 34 g fat (12 g sat. fat), 94 mg chol., 424 mg sodium, 86 g carb., 2 g fiber, 68 g sugars, 6 g pro.*

OLIVE OIL CAKE WITH ROASTED CITRUS

VANILLA BEAN-COCONUT CUPCAKES

PREP 40 minutes
COOK 20 minutes
BAKE 18 minutes at 375°F
COOL 45 minutes

1   14-oz. can unsweetened coconut milk
¾   cup butter
3   eggs
1   vanilla bean, split lengthwise
1¾   cups all-purpose flour
¼   cup ground macadamia nuts
2¼   tsp. baking powder
½   tsp. salt
1⅓   cups sugar
1   recipe Vanilla-Coconut Frosting
1   cup flaked coconut, lightly toasted (tip page 67)

1. In a medium saucepan bring coconut milk just to boiling; reduce heat. Simmer, uncovered, 20 to 30 minutes or until milk is reduced to 1⅓ cups; cool. Meanwhile, allow butter and eggs to stand at room temperature 30 minutes.

2. Preheat oven to 375°F. Line eighteen 2½-inch muffin cups with paper bake cups. Using the tip of a small sharp knife, scrape out seeds from vanilla bean. In a small bowl stir together flour, ground nuts, baking powder, and salt.

3. In a large bowl beat butter with a mixer on medium to high 30 seconds. Add sugar. Beat on medium to high 1 minute more, scraping sides of bowl occasionally.

4. Add eggs, one at a time, beating well after each addition. Stir in half the vanilla seeds; reserve remaining seeds for frosting. Alternately add flour mixture and

1 cup of the reduced coconut milk (reserve remaining coconut milk for frosting) to butter mixture, beating on low after each addition just until combined.

5. Spoon batter into prepared muffin cups, filling each about three-fourths full. Use the back of a spoon to smooth batter in cups. Bake 18 to 20 minutes or until tops spring back when lightly touched. Cool cupcakes in muffin cups on wire racks 5 minutes. Remove cakes from muffin cups. Cool completely on wire racks.

6. Pipe or spread Vanilla-Coconut Frosting onto tops of cupcakes. Sprinkle with toasted coconut. Makes 18 servings.

Vanilla-Coconut Frosting Allow 1 cup butter to stand at room temperature 30 minutes. In a large bowl beat butter with mixer on medium to high 30 seconds. Beat in reserved reduced coconut milk from cupcakes, reserved vanilla seeds from cupcakes, and ⅛ teaspoon salt. Gradually add 2½ cups powdered sugar, beating until fluffy.

PER SERVING 413 cal., 26 g fat (17 g sat. fat), 78 mg chol., 319 mg sodium, 44 g carb., 1 g fiber, 33 g sugars, 3 g pro.

VANILLA-SCENTED ORANGE CHEESECAKE

VANILLA-SCENTED ORANGE CHEESECAKE

PREP 30 minutes
STAND 30 minutes
BAKE 45 minutes at 375°F
COOL 45 minutes
CHILL 4 hours

2   8-oz. pkg. cream cheese
1   8-oz. carton sour cream
4   eggs
1½   cups finely crushed chocolate graham crackers or chocolate wafer cookies
¼   cup finely chopped pecans
1   Tbsp. sugar
½   cup butter, melted
1   vanilla bean, split lengthwise, or 1 tsp. vanilla bean paste
1   cup sugar
3   Tbsp. all-purpose flour
½   tsp. orange zest
    Few drops orange food coloring
½   cup orange marmalade
    Thinly sliced orange

1. Allow cream cheese, sour cream, and eggs to stand at room temperature 30 minutes. Meanwhile, for crust, in a medium bowl combine crushed graham

BOSTON CREAM CHEESECAKE

crackers, pecans, and 1 tablespoon sugar. Stir in melted butter. Press mixture onto the bottom and about 2 inches up the sides of an 8- or 9-inch springform pan; set aside.

2. Preheat oven to 375°F. If using vanilla bean, use the tip of a small sharp knife to scrape out seeds; set aside. In a large bowl beat cream cheese, sour cream, the 1 cup sugar, and the flour with a mixer on medium to high until combined. Using a fork, lightly beat eggs. Add eggs to cream cheese mixture, beating just until combined. Divide batter in half. Stir orange zest and food coloring into half the batter. Stir vanilla seeds or vanilla bean paste into remaining batter.

3. Pour orange batter into crust-lined pan, spreading evenly. Spoon vanilla batter over orange layer, gently spreading evenly. Place springform pan in a shallow baking pan.

4. Bake 45 to 55 minutes for the 8-inch pan, 40 to 50 minutes the 9-inch pan, or until a 2½-inch area around edge appears set when gently shaken.

5. Cool in pan on a wire rack for 15 minutes. Using a small sharp knife, loosen crust from sides of pan. Cool 30 minutes more. Remove sides of pan; cool cheesecake completely on wire rack.

6. Spoon marmalade over cheesecake; carefully spread to edge.* Cover and chill at least 4 hours or overnight before

serving. Top with fresh orange slices. Store in the refrigerator up to 3 days. Makes 12 servings.

* If the marmalade is too thick to spread, microwave 15 to 20 seconds to reach spreading consistency.

PER SERVING *431 cal., 28 g fat (15 g sat. fat), 134 mg chol., 293 mg sodium, 40 g carb., 1 g fiber, 28 g sugars, 6 g pro.*

BOSTON CREAM CHEESECAKE

PREP 30 minutes
STAND 30 minutes
BAKE 1 hour 15 minutes at 325°F
COOL 15 minutes
CHILL 4 hours 15 minutes

3	8-oz. pkg. cream cheese
3	eggs
1	pkg. 1-layer-size yellow cake mix
2	Tbsp. butter, melted
¾	cup sugar
1	tsp. vanilla
1	8-oz. carton sour cream
¾	cup heavy cream
6	oz. semisweet chocolate, finely chopped
2	Tbsp. butter, softened

1. Allow cream cheese and eggs to stand at room temperature 30 minutes. Meanwhile, preheat oven to 325°F. Grease the bottom of a 9-inch springform

pan; set aside. Prepare cake mix according to package directions, except add 2 tablespoons melted butter. Pour batter into prepared pan, spreading evenly. Bake 25 minutes.

2. Meanwhile, for cheesecake filling, in a large bowl beat cream cheese, sugar, and vanilla with a mixer on medium to high until smooth. Using a fork, lightly the beat eggs. Add eggs all at once, beating on low just until combined. Stir in sour cream. Carefully pour filling over cake layer in pan.

3. Bake 50 to 55 minutes or until a 2-inch area around the edge appears set when gently shaken. Cool in pan on a wire rack 15 minutes. Using a small sharp knife, loosen edges of cheesecake from sides of pan. Cool completely on wire rack. Remove sides of pan. Cover and chill at least 4 hours or overnight.

4. Before serving, in a small saucepan bring cream to simmering. Remove from heat. Add chocolate; stir until chocolate is melted and mixture is smooth. Stir in the 2 tablespoons softened butter. Chill 15 minutes or until slightly thickened, stirring once. Spoon chocolate over cheesecake to cover top and drizzle down sides. Makes 16 servings.

PER SERVING *347 cal., 24 g fat (12 g sat. fat), 102 mg chol., 272 mg sodium, 30 g carb., 1 g fiber, 20 g sugars, 5 g pro.*

BANANAS FOSTER CRÈMES BRÛLÉES

PREP 30 minutes
BAKE 25 minutes at 350°F
CHILL 1 hour
STAND 20 minutes

2½ cups heavy cream
½ cup milk
6 egg yolks
¾ cup sugar
2 tsp. vanilla
2 Tbsp. dark rum (optional)
1 Tbsp. butter
3 firm, ripe bananas, thinly sliced
⅓ cup sugar

1. Preheat oven to 350°F. For custards, in a medium-size heavy saucepan combine cream and milk; heat over medium heat just until bubbly around the edges.
2. Meanwhile, in a large bowl combine egg yolks, the ¾ cup sugar, and the vanilla. Beat with a wire whisk or rotary beater just until combined. Slowly whisk the hot cream mixture into the egg yolk mixture. If desired, stir in rum.
3. Place eight 6-ounce ramekins or custard cups in a large baking pan. Set pan on an oven rack. Divide egg yolk-cream mixture evenly among ramekins or cups. Pour enough hot water into the baking pan around the ramekins to reach halfway up the sides of ramekins.
4. Bake 25 to 30 minutes or until centers of custards appear set when carefully shaken. Remove custards from water bath; cool on a wire rack. Cover; chill 1 to 8 hours.
5. Before serving, let custards stand at room temperature 20 minutes. In a large skillet heat butter over medium heat until melted. Add banana slices; cook until bananas are golden brown, turning once. Arrange banana slices on custards.
6. Meanwhile, to caramelize sugar, place the ⅓ cup sugar in a heavy 8-inch skillet. Heat skillet over medium-high heat until sugar begins to melt, shaking skillet occasionally to heat sugar evenly. Do not stir. Once the sugar starts to melt, reduce heat to low and cook 3 minutes more or until all the sugar is melted and very light golden brown, stirring as needed with a wooden spoon.
7. Using a wooden spoon or fork, quickly drizzle caramelized sugar over custards. If sugar starts to harden in the skillet, return skillet to heat, stirring until melted. Before serving, let custards stand 2 to 3 minutes or until caramelized sugar is slightly set. Makes 8 servings.
PER SERVING 468 cal., 33 g fat (20 g sat. fat), 265 mg chol., 52 mg sodium, 41 g carb., 1 g fiber, 34 g sugars, 5 g pro.

BANANAS FOSTER CRÈMES BRÛLÉES

GANACHE-GLAZED PEANUT BUTTER TART

PREP 30 minutes
BAKE 10 minutes at 350°F
CHILL 4 hours
COOL 10 minutes
STAND 10 minutes

1 cup crushed chocolate wafer cookies
3 Tbsp. sugar
3 Tbsp. butter, melted
1½ cups half-and-half or light cream
2 Tbsp. all-purpose flour
¼ tsp. salt
3 egg yolks
⅓ cup sugar
½ cup creamy peanut butter
1 tsp. vanilla
4 oz. bittersweet chocolate, coarsely chopped
5 Tbsp. butter, cut up
1 Tbsp. light-color corn syrup
Chopped peanuts (optional)

1. Preheat oven to 350°F. For crust, in a medium bowl combine crushed chocolate cookies and the 3 tablespoons sugar. Drizzle with melted butter; toss to combine. Press crumb mixture onto the bottom and sides of an ungreased 9-inch tart pan that has a removable bottom. Bake 10 minutes or until set. Cool on a wire rack.
2. For filling, in a medium saucepan combine half-and-half, flour, and salt. Cook over medium heat until simmering, stirring frequently. In a small bowl combine egg yolks and ⅓ cup sugar. Gradually stir about half the hot mixture into egg yolk mixture. Return egg yolk mixture to saucepan. Cook and stir over medium heat until thickened and bubbly. Remove from heat. Whisk in peanut butter and vanilla until combined. Pour filling into crust-lined pan, spreading evenly. Cover and chill 3 hours.
3. For ganache, in a small saucepan combine chocolate and 5 tablespoons butter. Stir over low heat until melted. Remove from heat. Stir in corn syrup; cool 10 minutes.
4. Pour ganache over filling; tilt pan to allow ganache to flow evenly over top of tart. Cover and chill 1 to 24 hours.
5. Let stand at room temperature 10 minutes before serving. Using a small sharp knife, gently loosen edges of tart from sides of pan; remove sides of pan. To cut, dip sharp knife into hot water; dry knife. Quickly score top of tart with warm knife. Cut tart along score marks. If desired, sprinkle with chopped peanuts. Makes 16 servings.
PER SERVING 235 cal., 17 g fat (8 g sat. fat), 63 mg chol., 166 mg sodium, 19 g carb., 1 g fiber, 12 g sugars, 4 g pro.

GANACHE-GLAZED
PEANUT BUTTER TART

FRENCH TOAST
CASSEROLE WITH
CINNAMON-PEAR
COMPOTE

FRENCH TOAST CASSEROLE WITH CINNAMON-PEAR COMPOTE

PREP 30 minutes
CHILL 1 hour
BAKE 35 minutes at 375°F

5   eggs, lightly beaten
1   cup milk
⅓   cup granulated sugar
⅓   cup heavy cream
1   tsp. vanilla
¼   tsp. ground cinnamon
     Dash salt
6   1-inch slices dried whole wheat
     bread*
1   Tbsp. granulated sugar
2   Tbsp. butter
2   cups sliced peeled pears
¼   cup water
2   Tbsp. granulated sugar
1   Tbsp. brandy (optional)
¼   tsp. ground cinnamon
     Dash ground nutmeg
⅓   cup maple syrup
     Powdered sugar (optional)
     Whipped cream (optional)

1. For French toast, grease a 9×13-inch baking dish. In a large shallow dish combine the first seven ingredients (through salt), stirring until sugar is dissolved. Dip bread slices into egg mixture, turning to coat both sides. Arrange dipped slices in the prepared baking dish. Cover and chill 1 to 24 hours.
2. Preheat oven to 375°F. Sprinkle bread slices with the 1 tablespoon granulated sugar. Bake, uncovered, 35 minutes or until golden and puffed.
3. Meanwhile, in a medium saucepan melt butter over medium heat. Add the next six ingredients (through nutmeg). Cook and stir about 5 minutes or just until pears are tender. Gently stir in maple syrup.
4. If desired, sprinkle French toast with powdered sugar. Serve with pear compote and, if desired, whipped cream. Makes 6 servings.
*Tip To dry bread slices, arrange bread on a large baking sheet; cover loosely and let stand overnight. Or preheat oven to 300°F. Bake bread slices, uncovered, 5 minutes; cool.
PER SERVING *437 cal., 16 g fat (8 g sat. fat), 208 mg chol., 370 mg sodium, 63 g carb., 5 g fiber, 40 g sugars, 14 g pro.*

GIANDUJA CREAM PUFFS

PREP 30 minutes
COOL 10 minutes
BAKE 30 minutes at 400°F

1   cup water
½   cup butter
¼   tsp. salt
1   cup all-purpose flour
4   eggs
1½   cups heavy cream
¾   cup chocolate-hazelnut spread
      Powdered sugar (optional)
      Cocoa powder (optional)

1. Preheat oven to 400°F. Grease a large baking sheet; set aside.
2. In a medium saucepan combine the water, butter, and salt. Bring to boiling. Immediately add flour all at once; stir vigorously. Cook and stir until mixture forms a ball that doesn't separate. Cool

10 minutes. Add eggs, one at a time, beating well with a spoon after each addition.
3. Pipe* or drop 12 mounds of dough onto the prepared baking sheet. Bake 30 to 35 minutes or until golden and firm. Transfer to a wire rack; cool.
4. For filling, in a large bowl beat cream with a mixer on medium until soft peaks form (tips curl). Beat in chocolate-hazelnut spread on low just until combined.
5. Before serving, cut tops from pastry puffs; remove soft dough from inside. Pipe or spoon in filling. Replace tops. If desired, sprinkle with powdered sugar or cocoa powder. Makes 12 servings.
*Tip If you pipe the dough and filling, use a decorating bag fitted with a large star tip.
PER SERVING *333 cal., 26 g fat (14 g sat. fat), 123 mg chol., 159 mg sodium, 20 g carb., 1 g fiber, 11 g sugars, 5 g pro.*

GIANDUJA CREAM PUFFS

CIDER-BAKED STUFFED APPLES WITH SALTY CARAMEL SAUCE

PREP 30 minutes
SLOW COOK 5 hours (low) or 2½ hours (high)

4   baking apples, such as Pink Lady, Honeycrisp, or Braeburn, about 2½ to 2¾ inches in diameter
⅓   cup dried cranberries, chopped
¼   cup finely chopped walnuts
¼   cup packed brown sugar
1   cup apple cider or apple juice
1   tsp. lemon zest
2   Tbsp. lemon juice
3   inches stick cinnamon
1   Tbsp. butter, cut into four pieces
⅓   cup packed brown sugar
¼   cup heavy cream
¼   cup butter
1   Tbsp. light-color corn syrup
½   tsp. vanilla
½   tsp. coarse sea salt
    Vanilla or cinnamon ice cream (optional)

1. Core apples; peel a strip from the top of each apple. Place apples, top sides up, in a 3½- or 4-quart slow cooker. (If necessary, trim apples to stand upright in cooker.)

2. For the filling, in a small bowl combine cranberries, walnuts, and brown sugar. Spoon filling into centers of apples, patting in with a knife or narrow metal spatula. Combine apple cider, lemon zest, and lemon juice; pour around apples. Add stick cinnamon to liquid. Top each apple with a pat of butter.

3. Cover and cook on low 5 hours or on high 2½ hours.

4. Meanwhile, for caramel sauce, in a small heavy saucepan bring the ⅓ cup brown sugar, cream, butter, and corn syrup to boiling over medium-high heat, whisking occasionally; reduce heat to medium. Boil gently, uncovered, 2 minutes. Remove from heat. Stir in vanilla and sea salt. Cool to room temperature.

5. To serve, transfer warm apples to dessert dishes. Spoon some of the cooking liquid over apples. Serve with caramel sauce and, if desired, ice cream. Makes 4 servings.

PER SERVING 549 cal., 25 g fat (13 g sat. fat), 59 mg chol., 440 mg sodium, 80 g carb., 7 g fiber, 68 g sugars, 2 g pro.

HASSELBACK PEARS

PREP 15 minutes
ROAST 20 minutes at 400°F

2   8-oz. pears or apples, halved lengthwise and cored
2   tsp. packed brown sugar
¼   tsp. apple pie spice
2   Tbsp. butter, melted
⅓   cup packed brown sugar
¼   cup regular rolled oats
2   tsp. all-purpose flour
¼   tsp. apple pie spice
¼   cup butter
    Ice cream (optional)

1. Preheat oven to 400°F. Place pears, cut sides down, on a work surface. Arrange wooden skewers or chopsticks lengthwise on opposite sides of each pear half. Cut pear crosswise into ¼-inch slices, stopping when knife reaches skewers or chopsticks to prevent slicing all the way through.

2. Place pears in a shallow baking pan. Stir the 2 teaspoons brown sugar and ¼ teaspoon apple pie spice into 2 tablespoons melted butter; drizzle over pears. Cover with foil. Roast 10 minutes.

HASSELBACK PEARS

3. Meanwhile, in a small bowl combine the ⅓ cup packed brown sugar, oats, flour, and ¼ teaspoon apple pie spice. Cut in ¼ cup butter. Stuff oat mixture between fruit slices. Roast, uncovered, 10 minutes more. Drizzle with any pan drippings and, if desired, serve with ice cream. Makes 4 servings.

PER SERVING *303 cal., 18 g fat (11 g sat. fat), 46 mg chol., 144 mg sodium, 38 g carb., 3 g fiber, 3011 g sugars, 1 g pro.*

HOT COCOA SOUFFLE WITH COFFEE ICE CREAM

PREP 25 minutes
STAND 30 minutes
BAKE 40 minutes at 350°F

4	egg yolks
4	egg whites
3	Tbsp. sugar
2	Tbsp. unsweetened Dutch-process cocoa powder
¼	cup butter
½	cup sugar
½	cup unsweetened Dutch-process cocoa powder
¼	cup all-purpose flour
1	cup milk
2	Tbsp. sugar
1	quart coffee or other flavor ice cream

1. Allow egg yolks and egg whites to stand at room temperature 30 minutes.
2. Meanwhile, preheat oven to 350°F. Butter the sides of a 1½-quart oven-proof bowl or souffle dish. In a small bowl stir together the 3 tablespoons sugar and the 2 tablespoons cocoa powder. Sprinkle the prepared bowl with enough sugar-cocoa mixture to coat bottom and sides; set bowl and the remaining sugar-cocoa mixture aside.
3. In a medium saucepan melt the butter over medium heat. Stir in the ½ cup sugar, the ½ cup cocoa powder, and the flour. Add milk all at once. Cook and stir until thickened and bubbly. Remove from heat. In a medium bowl beat egg yolks with a fork until combined. Gradually stir milk mixture into beaten egg yolks. Set aside.
4. In a large bowl beat egg whites with a mixer on medium to high until soft peaks form (tips curl). Gradually add the 2 tablespoons sugar, beating until stiff peaks form (tips stand straight) and sugar is completely dissolved. Fold 1 cup of the beaten egg whites into egg yolk mixture to lighten. Fold egg yolk mixture into the remaining beaten egg whites. Transfer mixture to the prepared bowl.
5. Bake 40 to 45 minutes or until a knife inserted near center comes out clean. Immediately sprinkle top of baked souffle with the remaining sugar-cocoa mixture. Serve with scoops of ice cream or, if desired, place ice cream in center of souffle to serve. Makes 6 servings.
PER SERVING *484 cal., 24 g fat (13 g sat. fat), 178 mg chol., 206 mg sodium, 59 g carb., 2 g fiber, 50 g sugars, 11 g pro.*

HOT COCOA SOUFFLE WITH COFFEE ICE CREAM

FROSTY S'MORES

2. Place chocolate-almond ice cream in a large bowl and stir until softened and spreadable. Spread over graham cracker layer. Swirl fudge topping over chocolate-almond ice cream. Freeze 1 hour or until ice cream starts to firm.

3. Place salted caramel ice cream in a large bowl and stir until softened and spreadable. Spread salted caramel ice cream over chocolate and fudge layer. Cover and freeze overnight.

4. Preheat broiler. Quickly spread marshmallow creme over top of torte. Sprinkle with marshmallows and chocolate pieces.

5. Broil about 4 inches from heat for 30 to 60 seconds or just until marshmallows are golden. Cut torte into squares. Serve immediately. Cover and freeze to store. Makes 16 servings.

Make Ahead Prepare as directed through Step 3. Cover with plastic wrap, then with heavy foil. Freeze up to 1 month. To serve, continue as directed in Step 4.

PER SERVING 515 cal., 21 g fat (10 g sat. fat), 60 mg chol., 188 mg sodium, 79 g carb., 2 g fiber, 62 g sugars, 7 g pro.

FROSTY S'MORES

PREP 35 minutes
BAKE 10 minutes at 350°F
FREEZE 9 hours
BROIL 30 seconds

15	graham cracker squares
1	cup sliced almonds
2	Tbsp. sugar
6	Tbsp. butter, melted
1	qt. chocolate-almond or chocolate ice cream
1	cup hot fudge-flavor ice cream topping
1	qt. salted caramel or vanilla ice cream
1	13-oz. jar marshmallow creme
3	cups tiny marshmallows
1	cup miniature semisweet chocolate pieces

1. Preheat oven to 350°F. For crust, in a food processor combine graham crackers, almonds, and sugar. Cover and pulse until crackers are finely crushed. Add melted butter; cover and pulse until crumbs are moistened. Press mixture into the bottom of a 9×13-inch baking pan. Bake 10 to 12 minutes or until edges start to brown. Cool on a wire rack.

MALLOW-PRALINE SWEET POTATO PIE

PREP 45 minutes
BAKE 14 minutes at 450°F/45 minutes at 375°F
COOL 1 hour

1	recipe Pastry for a Single-Crust Pie (recipe page 95)
1²⁄₃	cups cooked, mashed orange sweet potatoes* or one 17.2-oz. can whole sweet potatoes, drained and mashed
⅓	cup granulated sugar
¼	cup pure maple syrup
1	tsp. finely chopped crystallized ginger or ½ tsp. ground ginger
½	tsp. ground cinnamon
½	tsp. freshly grated nutmeg or ¼ tsp. ground nutmeg
¼	tsp. ground allspice
⅛	tsp. salt
3	eggs, lightly beaten
1	cup buttermilk or sour milk**
2	Tbsp. butter
2	Tbsp. packed brown sugar
2	Tbsp. pure maple syrup
1	Tbsp. milk
½	cup chopped pecans
1	cup tiny marshmallows

1. Preheat oven to 450°F. Prepare Pastry for a Single-Crust Pie. On a lightly floured surface, use your hands to slightly flatten pastry. Roll pastry from center to edges into a circle about 12 inches in diameter. Wrap pastry circle around rolling pin. Unroll into a 9-inch pie plate. Ease pastry into pie plate without stretching it. Trim pastry to ½ inch beyond edge of pie plate. Fold under extra pastry even with plate edge. Crimp edge as desired. Generously prick bottom and sides of pastry with a fork. Line pastry with a double thickness of foil. Bake 8 minutes. Remove foil. Bake 6 to 8 minutes more or until golden. Cool on a wire rack.

2. Reduce oven temperature to 375°F. For filling, in a large bowl stir together sweet potatoes, granulated sugar, the ¼ cup maple syrup, the ginger, cinnamon, nutmeg, allspice, and salt. Add eggs; beat lightly with a fork just until combined. Gradually stir in buttermilk until thoroughly combined.

3. Place the baked pastry shell on a foil-lined baking sheet on an oven rack. Carefully pour filling into pastry shell. Bake 30 minutes.

4. Meanwhile, in a small saucepan melt the butter over medium heat. Gradually stir in brown sugar, the 2 tablespoons maple syrup, and the milk. Cook and stir until mixture comes to boiling. With pie on the oven rack, sprinkle partially baked pie with pecans and marshmallows. Carefully pour hot brown sugar mixture over the top. Bake 15 to 20 minutes more or until center appears set when shaken. Cool on a wire rack at least 1 hour. Cover and chill within 2 hours. Makes 8 servings.

*To prepare mashed sweet potatoes, in a medium-size covered saucepan cook about 18 oz. peeled, cubed sweet potatoes in enough boiling salted water to cover for 25 to 30 minutes or until tender. Drain potatoes. Mash potatoes with a potato masher or beat with a mixer on low until mashed.

**To make sour milk, combine 1 tablespoon lemon juice or vinegar and enough milk to equal 1 cup; let stand 5 minutes.

PER SERVING 468 cal., 22 g fat (8 g sat. fat), 104 mg chol., 333 mg sodium, 61 g carb., 3 g fiber, 31 g sugars, 8 g pro.

MALLOW-
PRALINE SWEET
POTATO PIE

HONEYED YOGURT
PUMPKIN PIE WITH
PISTACHIO-
COCONUT STREUSEL

HONEYED YOGURT PUMPKIN PIE WITH PISTACHIO-COCONUT STREUSEL

PREP 45 minutes
BAKE 14 minutes at 450°F/45 minutes at 350°F
COOL 2 hours

1   recipe Pastry for Single-Crust Pie
1   8-oz. pkg. cream cheese, softened
½   cup plain Greek yogurt
1   cup canned pumpkin
¼   cup honey
½   cup sugar
3   Tbsp. all-purpose flour
½   tsp. ground cinnamon
¼   tsp. salt
3   eggs, lightly beaten
1   tsp. vanilla
1   recipe Pistachio-Coconut Streusel

1. Preheat oven to 450°F. Prepare Pastry for a Single-Crust Pie. On a lightly floured surface, use your hands to slightly flatten pastry. Roll into a 12-inch circle. Transfer to a 9-inch pie plate, being careful not to stretch pastry. Trim to ½ inch beyond edge of plate; crimp edges as desired. Prick bottom and sides of pastry with a fork. Line pastry with a double thickness of foil. Bake 8 minutes; remove foil. Bake 6 to 8 minutes more or until golden. Cool on a wire rack.

2. Reduce oven temperature to 350°F. In a large bowl beat cream cheese and yogurt with a mixer on medium until smooth. Beat in pumpkin and honey. Stir in sugar, flour, cinnamon, and salt until combined. Stir in eggs and vanilla.

3. Pour filling into baked pastry shell. Sprinkle with Pistachio-Coconut Streusel. Cover edge of pie with foil.

4. Bake 45 to 55 minutes or until center is set. Cool on wire rack. Cover and chill within 2 hours. If desired, drizzle with additional honey. Makes 8 servings.

Pastry for Single-Crust Pie In a medium bowl stir together 1½ cups all-purpose flour and ¼ teaspoon salt. Using a pastry blender, cut in ¼ cup shortening and ¼ cup butter, cut up, until pea size. Sprinkle 1 tablespoon ice water over part of the flour mixture; toss gently with a fork. Push moistened pastry to side of bowl. Repeat moistening flour mixture, gradually adding ice water (¼ to ⅓ cup total) until mixture begins to come together. Gather dough into a ball, kneading gently just until it holds together.

Pistachio-Coconut Streusel In a medium bowl stir together 3 tablespoons all-purpose flour and 1 tablespoon each packed brown sugar and rolled oats. Using a pastry blender, cut in 2 tablespoons butter until mixture resembles coarse crumbs. Stir in 2 tablespoons each chopped pistachio nuts and flaked coconut.

PER SERVING *469 cal., 27 g fat (14 g sat. fat), 130 mg chol., 452 mg sodium, 49 g carb., 2 g fiber, 27 g sugars, 9 g pro.*

MAPLE, APPLE, AND CHEDDAR PIE

PREP 30 minutes
BAKE 1 hour at 375°F
COOL 1 hour

1   recipe Pastry for Double-Crust Pie
½   cup sugar
2   Tbsp. all-purpose flour
½   tsp. ground cinnamon
¼   tsp. salt
5   cups thinly sliced peeled apples (such as Jonathan or Macintosh)
1½ cups shredded white cheddar cheese (6 oz.)
¼   cup maple syrup
1   Tbsp. heavy cream
2   Tbsp. maple syrup
¼   cup chopped pecans, toasted (tip, page 105) (optional)

1. Preheat oven to 375°F. Prepare Pastry for a Double-Crust Pie. On a lightly floured surface, slightly flatten one dough portion. Roll dough from center to edge into a circle about 12 inches in diameter. Wrap pastry circle around the rolling pin; unroll into a 9-inch pie plate. Ease pastry into pie plate without stretching it.

2. For filling, in a large bowl stir together sugar, flour, cinnamon, and salt. Add apples; toss gently to coat. Add cheese and the ¼ cup maple syrup; toss gently to combine. Transfer filling to pastry-lined pie plate. Drizzle with cream. Trim pastry even with edge of pie plate.

3. Roll the remaining dough portion into a 12-inch circle. Cut slits in pastry to allow steam to escape. Place pastry circle on filling; trim pastry to ½ inch beyond edge of pie plate. Fold top pastry edge under bottom pastry. Crimp edge as desired. Cover edge of pie with foil to prevent overbrowning.

MAPLE, APPLE, AND CHEDDAR PIE

4. Bake 40 minutes. Remove foil. Bake 20 minutes more or until apples are tender and pastry is golden brown. Transfer to a wire rack. Brush with the 2 tablespoons maple syrup. If desired, sprinkle with pecans. Cool 1 hour. Serve slightly warm. Makes 8 servings.

Pastry for Double-Crust Pie In a large bowl stir together 2½ cups all-purpose flour and 1 teaspoon salt. Using a pastry blender, cut in ½ cup shortening and ¼ cup cut-up butter until pieces are pea size. Sprinkle 1 tablespoon ice water over part of the flour mixture; toss gently with a fork. Push moistened dough to side of bowl. Repeat with additional ice water, 1 tablespoon at a time (½ to ⅔ cup total), until all the flour mixture is moistened. Gather dough into a ball, kneading gently until it holds together. Divide dough in half. Shape each portion into a ball.

PER SERVING *524 cal., 26 g fat (12 g sat. fat), 40 mg chol., 540 mg sodium, 63 g carb., 2 g fiber, 0 g sugars, 29 g pro.*

Festive Cookies & Bars

Christmas season kicks into full gear when platters of homemade cookies are filled and shared with loved ones. Rolled and cut, sliced, shaped, dropped, or molded, these handheld bites of sweetness represent the most personal expression of holiday well wishes.

MERINGUE SNOWMEN,
PAGE 105

LEMON-WALNUT BISCOTTI

PISTACHIO-CRANBERRY ICEBOX COOKIES

PREP 25 minutes
CHILL 2 hours
BAKE 10 minutes at 350°F
COOL 1 minute

¾ cup unsalted butter, softened
⅓ granulated sugar
½ tsp. ground cinnamon
½ tsp. orange zest
¼ tsp. salt
1½ cups all-purpose flour
½ cup finely chopped pistachios
⅓ cup snipped dried cranberries
　 Coarse sanding sugar (optional)

1. In a large bowl beat butter with a mixer on medium to high 30 seconds. Add sugar, cinnamon, orange zest, and salt. Beat 3 minutes or until light and fluffy, scraping sides of bowl occasionally. Reduce speed to low. Beat in as much flour as you can, ½ cup at a time, with the mixer. Stir in any remaining flour. Stir in pistachios and cranberries. Use your hands to knead dough until smooth.
2. Divide dough in half. On waxed paper, shape each half into an 8½-inch log (about 1½ inches across). Lift and smooth waxed paper to shape the logs. If desired, roll logs in coarse sanding sugar. Wrap each log in plastic wrap or waxed paper. Chill 2 hours or until dough is firm enough to slice.
3. Preheat oven to 350°F. Line cookie sheets with parchment paper. Cut logs into ¼-inch slices. Rotate log while cutting to prevent flattening. (If dough gets too soft to slice, freeze briefly until firm enough to slice.) Place slices 1 inch apart on cookie sheets.
4. Bake 10 to 12 minutes or until edges are firm and just starting to brown. Cool on cookie sheets 1 minute. Remove cookies; cool on wire racks. Makes 18 cookies.
PER COOKIE *44 cal., 3 g fat (2 g sat. fat), 6 mg chol., 10 mg sodium, 4 g carb., 0 g fiber, 2 g sugars, 1 g pro.*

LEMON-WALNUT BISCOTTI

PREP 40 minutes
CHILL 15 minutes
BAKE 25 minutes at 325°F/12 minutes at 300°F
COOL 45 minutes

3 cups all-purpose flour
1 tsp. baking powder
½ tsp. salt
¼ tsp. baking soda
1 lemon
10 Tbsp. butter, softened
1⅓ cups granulated sugar
2 eggs
2 cups chopped walnuts
1 egg white, lightly beaten
3 Tbsp. turbinado sugar

1. Preheat oven to 325°F. Lightly grease 2 cookie sheets or line with parchment paper; set aside. In a large bowl stir together flour, baking powder, salt, and baking soda. Remove 4 teaspoons zest and 3 tablespoons juice from lemon.
2. In a large bowl beat butter with a mixer for 30 seconds. Add granulated sugar and lemon zest. Beat until combined, scraping sides of bowl occasionally. Beat in the 2 eggs, one at a time, until combined. Beat in lemon juice until combined. Beat in as much of the flour as you can with the mixer. Stir in any remaining flour. Stir in walnuts.
3. Turn dough out onto a lightly floured surface; divide dough into three portions. Shape each portion into a 10-inch loaf about 1½ inches wide. Place loaves about 3 inches apart on prepared cookie sheets; flatten slightly to about 2 inches wide. Brush with egg white. Sprinkle with turbinado sugar. Chill 15 minutes.
4. Bake 25 to 30 minutes or until firm and lightly browned. Reduce oven to 300°F. Cool on cookie sheets 45 minutes.
5. Transfer loaves to a cutting board. Using a serrated knife, cut each loaf diagonally into ½-inch slices. Place slices on ungreased cookie sheets.
6. Bake 7 minutes or until lightly browned. Turn slices over; bake 5 to 6 minutes more or until lightly browned and crisp. Remove slices cool on wire racks. Makes 36 biscotti.
PER BISCOTTI *105 cal., 6 g fat (2 g sat. fat), 15 mg chol., 56 mg sodium, 13 g carb., 1 g fiber, 6 g sugars, 2 g pro.*

PISTACHIO-
CRANBERRY ICEBOX
COOKIES

DOUBLE-MINT CHOCOLATE COOKIES

PREP 1 hour
CHILL 1 hour
BAKE 10 minutes per batch at 350°F
COOL 2 minutes

- ¾ cup butter, softened
- ½ cup granulated sugar
- ¼ cup packed brown sugar
- ½ tsp. baking soda
- ½ tsp. salt
- 1 egg
- ½ cup unsweetened cocoa powder
- 1½ cups all-purpose flour
- 24 small (1½- to 2-inch) chocolate-covered cream-filled mint patties, unwrapped and chilled
- 24 Kisses chocolate with mint (optional)
- 6 oz. white baking chocolate with cocoa butter, melted (optional) Striped round peppermint candies, crushed (optional)

1. In a large bowl beat butter with a mixer on medium to high 30 seconds. Add both sugars, baking soda, and salt. Beat on medium 2 minutes, scraping bowl as needed. Beat in egg until combined. Beat in the cocoa powder and as much of the flour as you can with the mixer. Stir in any remaining flour. Cover and chill dough about 1 hour or until easy to handle.
2. Preheat oven to 350°F. Line 2 baking sheets with parchment paper. Divide dough into 24 equal pieces (about 1½ tablespoon each). Working with one piece of dough at a time, cut the piece in half. Flatten each piece into a circle, just larger than the mint patty. Put a mint patty on one dough circle; place the other circle on top. Press dough around the peppermint patty to seal, making sure there are no holes. Place on prepared cookie sheet. Repeat with remaining dough and mint patties.
3. Bake 10 to 12 minutes or just until set. If desired, immediately top each cookie with a chocolate Kiss. Cool on cookie sheets 2 minutes. Remove; cool on wire racks. If desired, drizzle with melted white chocolate and sprinkle with crushed peppermint candies. Makes 24 cookies.
To Store Layer cookies between sheets of waxed paper in an airtight container; cover. Store at room temperature up to 3 days or freeze up to 3 months.
PER COOKIE *161 cal., 7 g fat (5 g sat. fat), 23 mg chol., 129 mg sodium, 24 g carb., 1 g fiber, 15 g sugars, 2 g pro.*

QUADRUPLE GINGER COOKIES

PREP 45 minutes
CHILL 1 hour
BAKE 10 minutes per batch at 350°F
COOL 1 minute

- 2 cups all-purpose flour
- 1½ to 2 tsp. ground ginger
- 1 tsp. baking soda
- 1 tsp. ground cinnamon
- ¾ tsp. salt
- ½ to 1 tsp. ground cloves
- ½ to ¾ cup finely snipped crystallized ginger
- ½ cup shortening
- ¼ cup butter, softened
- 1 cup packed light brown sugar
- ¼ cup dark molasses
- 1 egg
- 1 tsp. fresh ginger juice (optional)
- ¾ cup Ginger Sugar or granulated sugar

1. In a medium bowl stir together flour, ground ginger, baking soda, cinnamon, salt, and cloves. Stir in crystallized ginger.
2. In a large bowl beat shortening and butter with a mixer on medium to high 30 seconds. Add brown sugar. Beat until combined, scraping sides of bowl occasionally. Beat in molasses and egg until combined. Stir in fresh ginger juice, if using. Beat in as much of the flour as you can with the mixer. Stir in any remaining flour. Cover and chill dough 1 hour or until dough is easy to handle.
3. Preheat oven to 350°F. Place Ginger Sugar in a small bowl. Shape dough into 1-inch balls. Roll balls in Ginger Sugar. Place 1½ inches apart on lightly greased cookie sheets. Bake 10 to 12 minutes or until edges are set. Cool on cookie sheets 1 minute. Remove cookies; cool on wire racks. Makes 48 cookies.
Ginger Sugar In a small bowl stir together ¼ cup coarsely chopped fresh ginger and ¾ cup granulated sugar. Let stand 1 hour (sugar will clump slightly). Place mixture in a fine-mesh sieve set over a bowl; stir gently so sugar separates from ginger. Discard ginger.
PER COOKIE *86 cal., 3 g fat (0 g sat. fat), 7 mg chol., 74 mg sodium, 14 g carb., 0 g fiber, 0 g sugars, 1 g pro.*

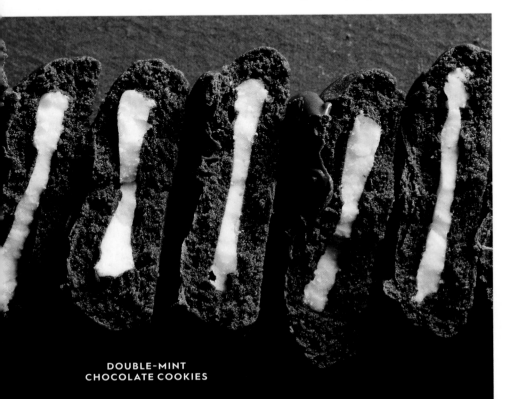

DOUBLE-MINT CHOCOLATE COOKIES

QUADRUPLE
GINGER
COOKIES

ISCHL
TARTS

ISCHL TARTS

PREP 45 minutes
CHILL 1 hour 45 minutes
BAKE 8 minutes per batch at 375°F

½ cup butter
1 cup powdered sugar
2 egg yolks
2 tsp. vanilla
¼ tsp. salt
¼ tsp. ground cinnamon
⅛ tsp. ground cloves
2¼ cups all-purpose flour
½ cup butter, softened
½ cup seedless red raspberry
    and/or apricot preserves

1. For spice dough, in a small saucepan cook ½ cup butter over medium heat for 12 minutes or until light brown. Pour into a medium bowl; chill just until firm (about 45 minutes). Beat with a mixer on medium 30 seconds. Beat in ½ cup of the powdered sugar, one of the egg yolks, 1 teaspoon of the vanilla, ⅛ teaspoon of the salt, the cinnamon, and cloves until fluffy. Beat in 1 cup of the flour.
2. For plain dough, in another medium bowl beat the ½ cup softened butter with the mixer on medium 30 seconds. Beat in the remaining powdered sugar, egg yolk, vanilla, and salt until fluffy. Beat in the remaining 1¼ cups flour. Cover and chill both doughs until easy to handle (about 1 hour).
3. Preheat oven to 375°F. On a lightly floured surface, roll spice dough to ⅛-inch thickness. Using 2½- to 3-inch fluted cookie cutters, cut out dough. Repeat with plain dough to make matching shapes. Using smaller cookie cutter, cut out shape(s) in plain dough. (Leave spice cutouts whole.) Place 1 inch apart on an ungreased cookie sheet.
4. Bake 8 minutes or until edges are lightly browned. Remove cookies; cool on wire racks.
5. Within 24 hours of serving time, spread preserves on bottoms of spice cookies, using about 1 teaspoon for each cookie. Top with plain cutout cookies, bottom sides down. Before serving, sprinkle lightly with additional powdered sugar. Makes 18 cookies.
PER COOKIE *207 cal., 11 g fat (7 g sat. fat), 48 mg chol., 127 mg sodium, 25 g carb., 1 g fiber, 11 g sugars, 2 g pro.*

SUGAR COOKIE CUTOUTS

SUGAR COOKIE CUTOUTS

PREP 40 minutes
CHILL 30 minutes
BAKE 7 minutes per batch at 375°F

1   cup butter, softened
1¼   cups granulated sugar
1½   tsp. baking powder
½   tsp. salt
2   eggs
2   tsp. vanilla
3   cups all-purpose flour
1   recipe Royal Icing (optional)

1. In a large mixing bowl beat butter on medium to high for 30 seconds. Add granulated sugar, baking powder, and salt. Beat until combined, scraping sides of bowl occasionally. Beat in eggs and vanilla until combined. Beat in as much of the flour as you can with the mixer. Stir in any remaining flour. Divide dough in half. Cover and chill dough 30 minutes or until easy to handle.
2. Preheat oven to 375°F. On a floured surface, roll half the dough at a time to ⅛- to ¼-inch thickness. Using a 2½- to 3-inch cookie cutter, cut into shapes. Place 1 inch apart on ungreased cookie sheets.
3. Bake 7 minutes or until edges are firm and bottoms are very light brown. Remove cookies; cool on wire racks. If desired, frost with Royal Icing. Makes about 52 cookies.
PER COOKIE *80 cal., 4 g fat (2 g sat. fat), 17 mg chol., 63 mg sodium, 10 g carb., 0 g fiber, 5 g sugars, 1 g pro.*

ROYAL ICING

START TO FINISH 15 minutes

1   lb. powdered sugar (about 4 cups)
3   Tbsp. meringue powder*
½   tsp. cream of tartar
½   cup warm water
1   tsp. vanilla

1. In a large bowl stir together powdered sugar, meringue powder, and cream of tartar. Add the ½ cup warm water and the vanilla. Beat with a mixer on low until combined. Beat on high 7 to 10 minutes or until icing is very stiff. If not using immediately, cover bowl with a damp paper towel; cover tightly with plastic wrap (icing will dry out quickly when exposed to air). Chill up to 48 hours. Stir before using. Makes 3 cups.
***Tip** Meringue powder is a mixture of pasteurized egg whites, sugar, and edible gums. It is the key ingredient to making Royal Icing dry quickly with a smooth, hard finish. Look for it in the baking aisle of large supermarkets or in the cake decorating department of hobby and crafts stores.
Glaze-Consistency Royal Icing Prepare Royal Icing as directed. Stir in additional vodka or other clear spirit, or warm water, about ½ teaspoon at a time, until icing is the consistency of a thick, spoonable paste. Use an artist brush to paint the cookies.
Food coloring options Paste, gel, and liquid color are all options for tinting icing or frostings. Paste offers a wide range of colors and is available at hobby stores. A toothpick works best for transferring the paste from the jar to the frosting. Because of their smooth consistency, gel colors are easy to stir into frosting. Find them online and at hobby stores. Liquid colors are found at most grocery stores in the spices aisle. This version comes in red, blue, green, and yellow. It takes some experimenting, but the colors can be mixed to create new colors.
PER 2 TBSP. *37 cal., 0 fat, 0 mg chol., 0 mg sodium, 9 g carb., 0 g fiber, 9 g sugars, 0 g pro.*

CREAMY WHITE FROSTING

START TO FINISH 10 minutes

1   cup shortening
1½   tsp. vanilla
½   tsp. almond extract
1   lb. powdered sugar (about 4 cups)
3   to 4 Tbsp. milk

1. In a large bowl beat shortening, vanilla, and almond extract with a mixer on medium 30 seconds. Slowly add about half of the powdered sugar, beating well. Add 2 tablespoons of the milk. Gradually beat in remaining powdered sugar and enough remaining milk to reach spreading consistency. You can freeze this frosting in a freezer container up to 3 months; thaw at room temperature before using. Makes about 3 cups.
PER 2 TBSP. *151 cal., 9 g fat (2 g sat. fat), 0 mg chol., 2 mg sodium, 10 g carb., 0 g fiber, 9 g sugars, 0 g pro.*

POWDERED SUGAR ICING

START TO FINISH 10 minutes

2   cups powdered sugar
½   tsp. vanilla
2   Tbsp. milk or orange juice
     Milk

1. In a small bowl combine powdered sugar, vanilla, and 2 tablespoons milk. Stir in additional milk, 1 teaspoon at a time, until icing reaches drizzling consistency. Makes about 1 cup.
Tip The difference between an icing that can be piped and one that can be spooned on as a glaze is a few drops of milk. Add milk slowly to Powdered Sugar Icing—a small amount goes a long way. If the icing is too soft, stir in a small amount of powdered sugar to thicken it.
PER 1 TBSP. *40 cal., 0 fat, 0 mg chol., 1 mg sodium, 10 g carb., 0 g fiber, 10 g sugars, 0 g pro.*

GINGERBREAD CUTOUTS

PREP 50 minutes
CHILL 1 hour
BAKE 6 minutes per batch at 375°F
COOL 1 minute

½ cup shortening
¼ cup butter, softened
½ cup granulated sugar
1 tsp. baking powder
1 tsp. ground ginger
½ tsp. baking soda
½ tsp. ground cinnamon
½ tsp. ground cloves
¼ tsp. salt
1 egg
½ cup molasses
1 Tbsp. cider vinegar
3 cups all-purpose flour

1. In a large bowl beat shortening and butter with a mixer on medium to high 30 seconds. Add sugar, baking powder, ginger, baking soda, cinnamon, cloves, and salt. Beat until combined, scraping bowl as needed. Beat in egg, molasses, and vinegar. Beat in as much of the flour as you can with the mixer. Stir in any remaining flour. Divide dough in half. Cover and chill 1 hour or until dough is easy to handle.

2. Preheat oven to 375°F. On a lightly floured surface, roll one dough portion and cut shapes as directed in variations, rerolling scraps as needed. Place cutouts 1 inch apart on ungreased cookie sheets.

3. Bake 6 to 8 minutes or until edges are firm. Cool on cookie sheet 1 minute. Remove cookies; cool on wire rack.

Gingerbread with Teddy Bear Roll dough to ¼-inch thickness. Cut with 3- to 4-inch people-shape cookie cutters. Place cookies on prepared cookie sheet. Place a teddy bear-shape graham cracker on the chest of each cookie. Wrap the cookie arms around the teddy bear, gently pressing the ends of two arms together. Bake and cool as directed. When cool, pipe faces and clothes with Powdered Sugar Icing (page 103). Makes about 24 cookies.

Loving Gingerbread Bears Line a baking sheet with parchment paper. Roll dough to ¼-inch thickness. Cut with 3- to 4-inch bear-shape cookie cutters.

Place cookies on prepared baking sheet. Use a 1-inch heart-shape cutter to cut a shape in the bear. Place 3 to 4 hard red or pink rectangular candies (such as Jolly Ranchers) in a plastic bag. Finely crush candies with a rolling pin. Lightly sprinkle a layer of crushed candies in the opening hole. Bake 6 minutes or until edges are firm. Cool on cookie sheet 15 minutes or until candy hardens. Remove; cool on wire racks. When cool, pipe with Powdered Sugar Icing (page 103). Makes about 24 cookies.

Reindeer Sticks Roll each half of dough to a 12×8-inch rectangle. Cut each into twenty-four 4×1-inch sticks. Place on cookie sheets. Bake and cool as directed. Place melted (room temperature) semisweet chocolate or canned chocolate frosting in a resealable plastic bag. Cut a very small hole in one corner. Pipe antler shapes and eyes on cookies. If desired, use chocolate or frosting to attach small red candies for noses. Makes 48 cookies (2 cookies per serving).

PER COOKIE *151 cal., 7 g fat (2 g sat. fat), 13 mg chol., 92 mg sodium, 21 g carb., 0 g fiber, 9 g sugars, 2 g pro.*

GINGERBREAD
CUTOUTS

SURPRISE SNOWBALLS

PREP 30 minutes
CHILL 30 minutes
BAKE 15 minutes per batch at 325°F

1   cup butter, softened
½   cup powdered sugar
1   Tbsp. hazelnut liqueur
1   tsp. vanilla
2   cups all-purpose flour
1½   cups finely chopped pecans or
      hazelnuts, toasted*
      Chocolate-covered caramels (Milk
      Duds) or bite-size unwrapped
      miniature chocolate-covered
      peanut butter cups
1   cup powdered sugar

1. In a large bowl beat butter with a mixer on medium to high 30 seconds. Add the ½ cup powdered sugar. Beat until combined, scraping bowl as needed. Beat in liqueur and vanilla. Beat in as much of the flour as you can with the mixer. Stir in any remaining flour and the pecans. Cover dough and chill 30 minutes or until easy to handle.
2. Preheat oven to 325°F. Shape dough into 1-inch balls. Press a chocolate-covered caramel into each ball, reshaping the ball around the candy to enclose it completely. Place balls about 2 inches apart on ungreased cookie sheets. Bake 15 minutes or until bottoms are light brown. Remove cookies; cool on wire racks.
3. Place the 1 cup powdered sugar in a large plastic bag. Add cooled cookies in batches to bag. Gently shake to coat. Makes 55 cookies.
*Tip To toast nuts, preheat oven to 350°F. Spread nuts in a shallow baking pan. Bake 5 to 10 minutes or until lightly browned, stirring pan once or twice.
PER COOKIE *94 cal., 6 g fat (3 g sat. fat), 9 mg chol., 35 mg sodium, 9 g carb., 0 g fiber, 5 g sugars, 1 g pro.*

MERINGUE SNOWMEN

(PHOTO, PAGES 96-97)

PREP 1 hour
BAKE 1 hour at 200°F
STAND 30 minutes

3   egg whites
½   tsp. vanilla or ¼ tsp. almond
      extract
¼   tsp. cream of tartar
⅛   tsp. salt
¾   cup sugar

SURPRISE SNOWBALLS

Orange jimmies
Melted chocolate

1. Preheat oven to 200°F. Line a cookie sheet with parchment paper.
2. In a large bowl beat egg whites, vanilla, cream of tartar, and salt with a mixer on medium until soft peaks form (tips curl). Gradually add sugar, about 1 tablespoon at a time, beating on high until stiff peaks form (tips stand straight).
3. Carefully spoon meringue into a new disposable pastry bag fitted with a large round tip. Pipe meringue into snowmen shapes about 1¼ inches tall, piping 2 to 3 balls larger at the bottom and gradually smaller toward the top. If desired,

carefully place one orange jimmy in each snowman for a nose. Dip a small spoon or butter knife in hot water and lightly round the snowmen tops.
4. Bake 1 hour or until meringues are set but not quite firm. Turn oven off and let meringue cookies stand in oven 30 minutes. Carefully remove cookies; cool on wire racks. If desired, spoon melted chocolate into a pastry bag and snip a very small hole in one corners. Pipe dots for eyes and pipe buttons and twig-like arms along the sides. Makes about 50 cookies.
PER COOKIE *13 cal., 0 fat, 0 mg chol., 9 mg sodium, 3 g carb., 0 g fiber, 3 g sugars, 0 g pro.*

S'MORES SPRITZ-WICHES

PREP 30 minutes
BAKE 6 minutes at 375°F

1½ cups butter, softened
1   cup granulated sugar
1   tsp. baking powder
1   tsp. ground cinnamon
1   egg
2   tsp. vanilla
3   cups all purpose flour
½   cup graham cracker crumbs
    Cinnamon-sugar (optional)
    Kisses milk chocolate miniatures
1   recipe Marshmallow Creme Filling

1. Preheat oven to 375°F. In a large bowl beat butter with a mixer on medium to high 30 seconds. Add granulated sugar, baking powder, and cinnamon. Beat until combined, scraping bowl as needed. Beat in egg and vanilla. Beat in as much of the flour as you can with the mixer. Stir in any remaining flour and the graham cracker crumbs.
2. Force unchilled dough through a cookie press fitted with a flower disk 1 inch apart onto ungreased cookie sheets. If desired, sprinkle cookies with cinnamon-sugar. Bake 6 minutes or until edges are firm but not brown. Immediately press a milk chocolate Kiss into centers of half the cookies. Remove cookies; cool on wire racks.
3. Spread Marshmallow Creme Filling on the bottoms of the plain cookies. Top with remaining cookies, bottom sides down. Makes 62 cookies.
Marshmallow Creme Filling In a large bowl beat 1 cup butter, softened, and 1 tablespoon vanilla with a mixer on medium 30 seconds. Add 4 cups powdered sugar and one 13-ounce jar marshmallow creme. Beat until well combined. If needed, beat in milk to reach spreading consistency.
PER COOKIE *162 cal., 8 g fat (5 g sat. fat), 23 mg chol., 77 mg sodium, 22 g carb., 0 g fiber, 15 g sugars, 1 g pro.*

**S'MORES
SPRITZ-
WICHES**

CANDY CANE ELFWICHES

PREP 45 minutes
CHILL 1 hour
BAKE 8 minutes per batch at 375°F

⅔ cup butter, softened
½ cup sugar
¼ tsp. salt
1 egg
1 tsp. vanilla
1½ cups all-purpose flour
   Red paste food coloring
1 recipe Peppermint Filling
   Finely crushed candy canes or
   peppermint candies (optional)

1. In a large bowl beat butter with a mixer on medium to high 30 seconds. Add sugar and salt. Beat until combined, scraping bowl as needed. Beat in egg and vanilla. Beat in as much of the flour as you can with the mixer. Stir in any remaining flour.
2. Divide dough in half. Leave one half plain. Tint the remaining half with of food coloring. Cover each portion and chill about 1 hour or until dough is easy to handle.
3. Preheat oven to 375°F. Shape each portion of dough into ½-inch balls. Roll together one plain ball and one red ball. Place on an ungreased cookie sheet. Press with the bottom of a sugared glass to about ¼-inch thickness. Repeat with remaining dough, placing balls 2 inches apart on cookie sheet. Bake 8 to 10 minutes or until edges are light brown. Remove cookies; cool on wire rack.
4. Spread Peppermint Filling on bottoms of half the cookies, using 2 teaspoons for each cookie. Top with the remaining cookies, bottom sides down. If desired, roll edges of frosting in crushed candy. Makes 20 cookies.
Peppermint Filling In a medium bowl beat ⅓ cup butter, softened, with a mixer on medium to high 30 seconds. Beat in 1 tablespoon milk and ¼ teaspoon peppermint extract. Gradually beat in 2 cups powdered sugar until combined. Beat in additional milk, 1 teaspoon at a time, until filling reaches piping consistency.
PER COOKIE *187 cal., 10 g fat (6 g sat. fat), 34 mg chol., 115 mg sodium, 24 g carb., 0 g fiber, 17 g sugars, 1 g pro.*

CANDY CANE
ELFWICHES

ANGEL WINGS

PREP 20 minutes
FREEZE 2 hours
BAKE 15 minutes per batch at 375°F

1   8-oz. pkg. cream cheese, softened
½   cup powdered sugar
¼   cup all-purpose flour
2   tsp. vanilla bean paste or vanilla
1   tsp. orange zest
1   17.3-oz. pkg. frozen puff pastry,
     thawed
     Powdered sugar

1. For filling, in a medium bowl beat cream cheese, powdered sugar, flour, orange zest, and vanilla bean paste with a mixer on low to medium until smooth.
2. On a lightly floured surface, unfold one pastry sheet. Roll to a 10-inch square. Spread half the filling on dough, leaving a ½-inch border on two opposite edges. Roll up from each of these edges, scroll fashion, to meet in the center. Brush seam with water where dough spirals meet; lightly press together. Repeat with the remaining filling and dough. Wrap each roll in plastic wrap and place on a tray or cookie sheet. Freeze 2 hours or until firm.
3. Preheat oven to 375°F. Line cookie sheets with parchment paper; set aside. Using a serrated knife, cut rolls into ¼-inch slices. Place slices 2 inches apart on the prepared cookie sheets. Bake 15 to 17 minutes or until edges are firm and bottoms are brown. Remove; cool on wire racks. Before serving, use a fine-mesh sieve to sprinkle cookies with powdered sugar. Makes 60 cookies.
PER COOKIE *65 cal., 4 g fat (2 g sat. fat), 4 mg chol., 32 mg sodium, 6 g carb., 0 g fiber, 1 g sugars, 1 g pro.*

ROCKY ROAD SUGAR COOKIE CUPS

PREP 1 hour
BAKE 10 minutes per batch at 350°F
COOL 5 minutes

     Nonstick cooking spray
1   cup butter, softened
1¼   cups sugar
1½   tsp. baking powder
½   tsp. salt
2   eggs
2   tsp. vanilla
1   tsp. orange zest or almond extract
     (optional)
3   cups all-purpose flour
1   13-oz. jar marshmallow creme
     Chocolate ice cream topping
     Chopped peanuts

1. Coat 1¾-inch muffin cups with cooking spray. In a large bowl beat butter with a mixer on medium 30 seconds. Beat in sugar, baking powder, and salt, scraping bowl as needed. Beat in eggs, vanilla, and, if desired, orange zest. Beat in as much of the flour as you can with the mixer. Stir in any remaining flour. If necessary, cover and chill dough 30 minutes or until easy to handle.
2. Preheat oven to 350°F. Shape dough into 1¼-inch balls. Press dough balls into bottom and up sides of prepared muffin cups.
3. Bake 10 to 12 minutes or until edges are lightly browned. Repress the centers with the rounded side of a measuring spoon. Cool in pans 5 minutes. Remove cups from pans and cool completely on wire racks.
4. Place marshmallow creme in a resealable plastic bag with a hole snipped from one corner. Squeeze the creme into each cookie cup. Drizzle with ice cream topping; sprinkle with peanuts. Makes 64 cookies.
PER COOKIE *93 cal., 3 g fat (2 g sat. fat), 13 mg chol., 63 mg sodium, 15 g carb., 0 g fiber, 8 g sugars, 1 g pro.*

ANGEL WINGS

ROCKY ROAD SUGAR
COOKIE CUPS

ORANGE CREAM
SUGAR COOKIE
BARS

ORANGE CREAM SUGAR COOKIE BARS

PREP 35 minutes
PREP 20 minutes at 350°F

    Nonstick cooking spray
3   cups all-purpose flour
1   tsp. baking powder
1   Tbsp. cornstarch
½   tsp. salt
1   cup butter, softened
½   cup granulated sugar
½   cup packed brown sugar
1   egg
1½ tsp. vanilla bean paste or vanilla extract
2   Tbsp. orange zest
1   recipe White Chocolate Frosting

1. Preheat oven to 350°F. Line a 9×13-inch baking pan with foil, extending foil over edges of pan. Coat foil with nonstick cooking spray. Set pan aside. In a bowl combine flour, baking powder, cornstarch, and salt.

2. In a large bowl beat butter with a mixer on medium 30 seconds. Add both sugars. Beat on medium to high until light and fluffy. Beat in egg, vanilla, and orange zest. Beat in flour mixture. Transfer dough to prepared baking pan. With lightly floured fingers, spread dough in pan.

3. Bake 20 to 25 minutes or until edges are light golden brown. Cool completely on a wire rack. Spread White Chocolate Frosting over cooled bars. Use edges of foil to lift uncut bars out of pan. Transfer to a cutting board. Cut into bars. If desired, just before serving, sprinkle with additional orange zest. Makes 48 bars.

White Chocolate Frosting In a small heavy saucepan combine 2 ounces white baking chocolate, chopped, and 2 tablespoons heavy cream. Stir over low heat until chocolate is melted and mixture is smooth. Remove from heat and cool 5 minutes. In a large bowl beat ½ cup softened butter with a mixer on medium 30 seconds. Beat in 2 cups powdered sugar until light and fluffy. Add melted white chocolate mixture, 1 teaspoon vanilla bean paste or vanilla extract, and a pinch salt, beating on low until combined. Beat in 2 tablespoons heavy cream, 1 tablespoon at a time. Beat on medium until very light and fluffy.

PER BAR *129 cal., 7 g fat (4 g sat. fat), 21 mg chol., 87 mg sodium, 16 g carb., 0 g fiber, 10 g sugars, 1 g pro.*

LIME-MACAROON BARS

LIME-MACAROON BARS

PREP 20 minutes
BAKE 40 minutes at 350°F

    Nonstick cooking spray
2   limes
1   cup butter, softened
1¾ cups sugar
2   tsp. baking powder
½   tsp. salt
3   eggs
1   tsp. vanilla
3   cups all-purpose flour
1   egg white, lightly beaten
1   14-oz. pkg. flaked coconut
1   14-oz. can sweetened condensed milk

1. Preheat oven to 350°F. Line a 9×13-inch baking pan with foil, extending foil over edges of pan. Lightly coat foil with cooking spray. Set pan aside. Remove 1 tablespoon zest and squeeze 3 tablespoons juice from the limes.

2. For crust, in a large bowl beat butter with a mixer on medium 30 seconds. Add sugar, baking powder, salt, and lime zest. Beat until light and fluffy, scraping bowl as needed. Beat in the 3 eggs, vanilla, and lime juice until combined. Beat in flour. Spread batter in the prepared pan. Bake 15 minutes or until set and dry. Remove from oven.

3. Meanwhile, in a large bowl combine the egg white, coconut, and condensed milk. Spoon coconut mixture evenly over hot crust. Bake 25 minutes more or until topping is golden brown. Cool bars in pan on a wire rack. Use edges of foil to lift uncut bars out of pan. Place on a cutting board. Cut into bars. Makes 48 bars.

PER BARS *161 cal., 7 g fat (5 g sat. fat), 25 mg chol., 115 mg sodium, 22 g carb., 1 g fiber, 15 g sugars, 2 g pro.*

DATE-ORANGE BARS

1 cup packed brown sugar
½ cup granulated sugar
½ cup pure maple syrup
2 eggs
2 tsp. vanilla
2 cups all-purpose flour
1 tsp. baking powder
½ tsp. salt
¼ tsp. baking soda
1 recipe Maple Icing

1. Preheat oven to 350°F. Line a 9×13-inch pan with foil, extending foil over edges of pan. Lightly coat foil with cooking spray. In a saucepan melt 1 tablespoon butter over medium heat. Add apples; cook 12 minutes or until tender, stirring occasionally. Remove apples from saucepan.
2. In the same saucepan melt the remaining butter over medium heat. Remove from heat. Stir in brown sugar, granulated sugar, and maple syrup until smooth. Stir in eggs until combined; stir in vanilla. Stir in flour, baking powder, salt, and baking soda. Stir in cooked apples. Spread batter in prepared pan.
3. Bake 25 to 30 minutes or until lightly browned and edges are puffed. Cool in pan on a wire rack. Spread Maple Icing over bars. Let stand until icing is set. Use edges of foil to lift uncut bars out of pan. Transfer to a cutting board. Cut into bars. Makes 36 bars.
Maple Icing In a small bowl stir together 2 cups powdered sugar; ¼ cup pure maple syrup; and 2 tablespoons butter, melted. Stir in milk (about 2 tablespoons) to make a thin spreading consistency.
PER BAR *152 cal., 5 g fat (3 g sat. fat), 22 mg chol., 97 mg sodium, 27 g carb., 0 g fiber, 20 g sugars, 1 g pro.*

DATE-ORANGE BARS

PREP 25 minutes
BAKE 30 minutes at 350°F

2 eggs, slightly beaten
½ cup orange juice
½ cup butter, melted
1 cup all-purpose flour
½ cup sugar
1 tsp. baking powder
½ tsp. salt
1 8-oz. pkg. pitted whole dates, snipped
¾ cup chopped walnuts
Orange Icing (optional)

1. Preheat oven to 350°F. In a bowl combine eggs, orange juice, and butter.
2. In a large bowl combine flour, sugar, baking powder, and salt. Stir in dates and walnuts. Toss lightly with a fork to coat dates and nuts with the flour mixture. Add egg mixture; mix well.

3. Spread batter into a greased 8×8-inch baking pan. Bake 30 minutes or until a toothpick inserted in center comes out clean. Cool in pan on a wire rack. If desired, drizzle bars with Orange Icing. Makes 16 bars.
PER BAR *192 cal., 11 g fat (0 g sat. fat), 43 mg chol., 168 mg sodium, 24 g carb., 2 g fiber, 0 g sugars, 3 g pro.*
Orange Icing In a bowl stir together ½ cup powdered sugar and 1 to 2 teaspoons frozen orange juice concentrate to drizzling consistency.

MAPLE-APPLE BLONDIES

PREP 35 minutes
BAKE 25 minutes at 350°F

Nonstick cooking spray
¾ cup butter
2 medium apples, peeled (if desired), cored, and chopped (1¾ cups)

CRÈME BRÛLÉE CHEESECAKE COOKIE BARS

PREP 30 minutes
BAKE 35 minutes at 350°F
COOL 1 hour
CHILL 2 hours

Nonstick cooking spray
1 cup butter, softened
1 cup sugar
2 tsp. vanilla
2 cups all-purpose flour
3 8-oz. pkg. cream cheese, softened
1 cup sugar
2 Tbsp. all-purpose flour
⅓ cup sour cream

**CRÈME BRÛLÉE CHEESECAKE
COOKIE BARS**

1   Tbsp. vanilla
4   eggs, lightly beaten
¼   cup sugar

1. Preheat oven to 350°F. Line a 9×13-inch baking pan with foil, extending foil over edges of pan. Lightly coat foil with cooking spray. In a bowl beat butter with a mixer on medium 30 seconds. Add 1 cup sugar and the 2 teaspoons vanilla. Beat until combined. Add the 2 cups flour; beat until crust comes together. Press into pan.

2. In an extra-large bowl beat cream cheese with mixer on medium until smooth. Add 1 cup sugar and 2 tablespoons flour; beat until combined. Beat in sour cream and 1 tablespoon vanilla on low just until combined. Beat in eggs on low. Pour over crust.
3. Bake 35 minutes or until edges are puffed and center is nearly set. Cool completely on a wire rack. Cover and chill at least 2 hours.
4. Just before serving, sprinkle uncut bars with ¼ cup sugar. Use a culinary torch to

brown the sugar on bars. Use edges of foil to lift uncut bars out of pan. (Or use edges of foil to lift uncut bars from pan. Place on a baking sheet. Wrap foil around edges. Broil 5 inches from heat for 3 minutes or until sugar is browned, rotating pan often to brown sugar evenly. Cool.) Cut into bars. Makes 36 bars.
PER BAR *200 cal., 13 g fat (7 g sat. fat), 54 mg chol., 109 mg sodium, 19 g carb., 0 g fiber, 13 g sugars, 3 g pro.*

BOOZY EGGNOG BARS

PREP 35 minutes
BAKE 25 minutes at 350°F
CHILL 4 hours

    Nonstick cooking spray
1¾ cups finely crushed vanilla wafers
¼ cup finely chopped walnuts
1 Tbsp. sugar
⅓ cup butter, melted
2 8-oz. pkg. cream cheese, softened
⅔ cup eggnog
½ cup sugar
2 Tbsp. dark rum or eggnog
½ tsp. freshly grated nutmeg or
    ¼ tsp. ground nutmeg
2 tsp. vanilla
3 eggs, lightly beaten
    Freshly grated nutmeg (optional)

1. Preheat oven to 350°F. Line a 9×13-inch baking pan with foil, extending foil over edges of pan. Lightly coat foil with cooking spray. In a bowl stir together crushed wafers, walnuts, 1 tablespoon sugar, and butter until evenly coated. Press mixture firmly into prepared pan.

2. In a large bowl beat cream cheese with a mixer on medium until smooth. Beat in eggnog, the ½ cup sugar, rum, nutmeg, and vanilla until thoroughly combined. Stir in eggs. Pour cream cheese mixture over crust in pan. If desired, lightly dust with additional freshly grated nutmeg.

3. Bake 25 to 30 minutes or until edges are puffed and center is set. Cool completely on wire rack. Chill 4 to 24 hours before serving. To serve, use edges of foil to lift uncut bars out of pan. Transfer to a cutting board. Cut into bars. Makes 36 bars.

PER BAR *114 cal., 8 g fat (4 g sat. fat), 36 mg chol., 82 mg sodium, 8 g carb., 0 g fiber, 6 g sugars, 2 g pro.*

COPYCAT MUSKETEER BARS

PREP 25 minutes
CHILL 1 hour

    Nonstick cooking spray
1 11.5-oz. pkg. milk chocolate pieces
18 to 21 chocolate wafer cookies
1 13-oz. jar chocolate spread
2 Tbsp. butter, melted
2 Tbsp. malted milk powder
2 7-oz. jars marshmallow creme

1. Line a 9×13-inch pan with foil, extending foil over edges of pan. Lightly coat foil with cooking spray. In a small bowl microwave half the chocolate pieces 1 minute or until melted, stirring every 30 seconds. Spread evenly on bottom of prepared pan. Arrange chocolate wafer cookies in a single layer on chocolate layer, breaking cookies as needed to fit. Chill 30 minutes or until chocolate is set.

2. Meanwhile, in a large bowl combine chocolate spread, butter, and malted milk powder. Stir in marshmallow creme. Microwave 30 seconds, stirring after 15 seconds. Stir until fully combined. With lightly greased hands or lightly greased rubber spatula, pat mixture evenly over cookie layer in pan.

3. In a small bowl microwave the remaining chocolate pieces 1 minute or until melted, stirring every 30 seconds. Immediately spread melted chocolate evenly over marshmallow layer. Chill 30 minutes or until topping is firm. Use edges of foil to lift uncut bars out of pan.

BOOZY EGGNOG BARS

COPYCAT MUSKETEER BARS

Transfer to a cutting board. Cut into bars. Makes 36 bars.

PER BAR *163 cal., 7 g fat (3 g sat. fat), 6 mg chol., 57 mg sodium, 23 g carb., 1 g fiber, 18 g sugars, 2 g pro.*

CHOCOLATE-SWIRLED PUMPKIN BARS

PREP 25 minutes
BAKE 30 minutes at 350°F

2   cups all-purpose flour
1½   cups sugar
2   tsp. baking powder
2   tsp. ground cinnamon
1   tsp. baking soda
½   tsp. salt
¼   tsp. ground cloves
1   15-oz. can pumpkin
4   eggs, lightly beaten
1   cup vegetable oil
1   cup miniature semisweet
     chocolate pieces
1   8-oz. package cream cheese,
     softened
⅓   cup sugar
1   egg
1   Tbsp. milk

1. Preheat oven to 350°F. Line a 15×10-inch baking pan with foil, extending foil over edges. In a large bowl stir together first seven ingredients (through cloves). Stir in pumpkin, the 4 eggs, and oil until combined. Spread batter in prepared pan.
2. In a small bowl microwave ½ cup of the chocolate pieces 1 minute or until melted, stirring after 30 seconds. In a medium bowl beat cream cheese and ⅓ cup sugar with a mixer on medium until combined. Beat in 1 egg, milk, and melted chocolate. Spoon over pumpkin batter. Using a narrow metal spatula or table knife, swirl slightly to marble. Sprinkle with remaining ½ cup chocolate pieces.
3. Bake 30 to 35 minutes or until puffed and a toothpick comes out clean. Cool in pan on a wire rack. Using foil, lift uncut bars out of pan. Cut into bars. Makes 24 bars.

PER BAR *286 cal., 16 g fat (4 g sat. fat), 50 mg chol., 192 mg sodium, 32 g carb., 0 g fiber, 0 g sugars, 4 g pro.*

CHOCOLATE-SWIRLED PUMPKIN BARS

COCONUT JOY CANDY BARS

PREP 20 minutes
BAKE 32 minutes at 350°F
COOL 1 hour 30 minutes
CHILL 1 hour

Nonstick cooking spray
¾ cup butter, melted
2 cups sugar
2 tsp. vanilla
3 eggs, lightly beaten
1¼ cups all-purpose flour
½ cup unsweetened cocoa powder
1 tsp. baking powder
½ tsp. salt
4 cups flaked coconut
1 14-oz. can sweetened condensed milk

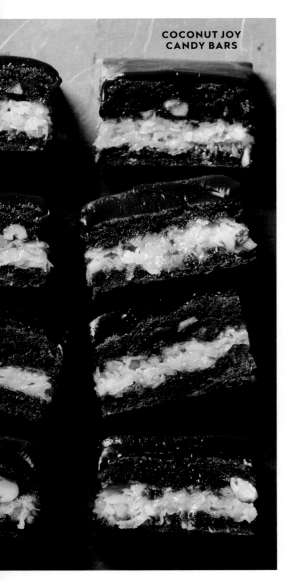

COCONUT JOY CANDY BARS

½ tsp. almond extract
½ cup chopped almonds, toasted (tip, page 105)
1 recipe Milk Chocolate Ganache

1. Preheat oven to 350°F. Line a 9×13-inch baking pan with foil, extending foil over edges of pan. Lightly coat foil with cooking spray. In a large bowl stir together melted butter, sugar, and 1 teaspoon of the vanilla until combined. Stir in eggs until combined.
2. In another bowl combine flour, cocoa powder, baking powder, and salt. Add flour mixture to butter mixture and stir until combined. Spread half the batter into the prepared pan. Bake 12 minutes or just until set. Cool on a wire rack 30 minutes.
3. Meanwhile, for filling, in a large bowl combine coconut, condensed milk, the remaining 1 teaspoon vanilla, and the almond extract.
4. Spread filling over baked chocolate layer; sprinkle with almonds. Carefully spread remaining chocolate batter over filling. Bake 20 to 25 minutes or until chocolate layer is set. Cool in pan on a wire rack.
5. Spoon Milk Chocolate Ganache over cooled bars, spreading evenly. Chill at least 1 hour or until ganache is firm. Use edges of foil to lift uncut bars out of pan. Transfer to a cutting board. Cut into bars. Makes 48 bars.

Milk Chocolate Ganache Pour one 11.5-ounce package milk chocolate pieces into a medium bowl and set aside. In a small saucepan bring ¾ cup heavy cream just to boiling. Immediately pour cream over chocolate in bowl. Let stand, without stirring, 5 minutes. Stir until smooth.

To Store Place bars in a single layer in an airtight container; cover. Store in the refrigerator up to 3 days or freeze up to 3 months.

PER BAR *187 cal., 10 g fat (6 g sat. fat), 28 mg chol., 96 mg sodium, 24 g carb., 1 g fiber, 19 g sugars, 3 g pro.*

SNICKEROONI BARS

PREP 30 minutes
BAKE 12 minutes at 350°F
FREEZE 30 minutes
CHILL 2 hours

Nonstick cooking spray
1 14.3-oz. pkg. chocolate sandwich cookies with white filling (36 cookies)
⅓ cup butter, melted
1¼ cups sugar
⅓ cup butter, cut up
1 5-oz. can (⅔ cup) evaporated milk
1 7-oz. jar marshmallow creme
¼ cup creamy peanut butter
1¾ cups cocktail peanuts or salted cashews, chopped
1 14-oz. bag vanilla caramels (about 50), unwrapped
1½ cups milk chocolate pieces (8 oz.)

1. Preheat oven to 350°F. Line a 9×13-inch baking pan with foil, extending foil over edges of pan. Lightly coat foil with cooking spray. Place cookies in a food processor. Cover and process until very finely chopped. In a bowl combine cookie crumbs and ⅓ cup melted butter. Firmly press crumb mixture into the prepared pan. Bake 12 minutes or until set. Cool in pan on a wire rack.
2. For the nougat, in a medium saucepan combine sugar, ⅓ cup butter, and ½ cup of the evaporated milk. Bring to boiling over medium-high heat, stirring to dissolve sugar. Reduce heat to medium. Simmer, uncovered, 10 minutes. Remove saucepan from heat. Stir in marshmallow creme and peanut butter. Stir in the chopped nuts. Pour nougat over crust in the baking pan, carefully spreading to edges. Place pan in freezer 20 minutes while preparing caramel layer.
3. For caramel layer, place caramels and the remaining evaporated milk (about 2 tablespoons) in a medium bowl. Microwave 1½ to 2 minutes or until caramels are melted, stirring every 30 seconds. Pour caramel mixture over nougat layer in pan, carefully spreading to edges. Return pan to freezer for 10 to 15 minutes while preparing last layer.
4. In a small bowl microwave chocolate pieces for 1 minute or until melted and smooth, stirring every 30 seconds. Pour chocolate mixture over caramel layer, spreading to edges. Cover and chill about 2 hours or until firm. Use edges of foil to lift uncut bars out of pan, cut into bars. Makes 60 bars.

PER BAR *154 cal., 8 g fat (3 g sat. fat), 7 mg chol., 86 mg sodium, 20 g carb., 1 g fiber, 14 g sugars, 2 g pro.*

FRESHLY BAKED

SNICKEROONI
BARS

fresh baked

EASY MONSTER
COOKIE BARS,
PAGE 122

Gifts from the Kitchen

Express gratitude to friends, colleagues, teachers, and party hosts with this selection of bars, breads, cakes, and cookies. Presenting the homemade treats in clever packaging magnifies the delight of giving and receiving.

**ALMOND SPRITZ,
PAGE 126**

**FROSTED
SNOWMAN CAKE**

FROSTED
SNOWMAN CAKE

PREP 25 minutes
BAKE 30 minutes at 350°F

1⅓ cups all-purpose flour
⅔ cup sugar
2 tsp. baking powder
⅔ cup milk
¼ cup butter, softened
1 egg
1 tsp. vanilla
  Canned white frosting
2 chocolate sandwich cookies with white filling
5 mini chocolate sandwich cookies with white filling
  Orange candy-coated milk chocolate pieces

1. Preheat oven to 350°F. Grease a 9-inch round foil pan; set pan aside.
2. In a bowl stir together flour, sugar, and baking powder. Add milk, butter, egg, and vanilla. Beat with a mixer on low until combined. Beat on medium 1 minute more. Spread batter in prepared pan.
3. Bake 30 minutes or until a wooden toothpick inserted near center comes out clean. Cool cake in pan on a wire rack.
4. Frost cooled cake with frosting. Decorate cake to look like a snowman face using large cookies for eyes, mini cookies for mouth, and candy- coated milk chocolate pieces for a nose. Makes 8 servings.
PER SERVING *480 cal., 17 fat (6 g sat. fat), 40 mg chol., 330 mg sodium, 78 g carb., 1 g fiber, 55 g sugars, 4 g pro.*

CHOCOLATE CHIP COOKIE DUNKERS

PREP 45 minutes
BAKE 25 minutes at 350°F/20 minutes at 325°F
COOL 1 hour
STAND 1 hour

¼	cup butter, softened
¼	cup shortening
½	cup packed brown sugar
¼	cup granulated sugar
¼	tsp. baking soda
1	egg
1	tsp. vanilla
1¼	cups all-purpose flour
½	cup miniature semisweet chocolate pieces
½	cup chopped walnuts or pecans (optional)
6	oz. semisweet chocolate, chopped (optional)
1	Tbsp. shortening (optional)

1. Preheat oven to 350°F. Line a 9×9-inch baking pan with foil, extending edges over sides of pan.

2. Beat butter and ¼ cup shortening in a medium bowl with a mixer on medium for 30 seconds. Add brown sugar, granulated sugar, and baking soda. Beat until combined, scraping sides of bowl occasionally. Beat in egg and vanilla until combined. Beat in as much of the flour as you can with the mixer. Stir in any remaining flour. Stir in miniature semisweet chocolate pieces and, if desired, nuts.

3. Press dough into prepared baking pan. Bake 25 to 30 minutes or until golden brown and center is set. Cool in pan on a wire rack 1 hour. Reduce oven temperature to 325°F.

4. Use foil to lift cookie out of pan. Transfer to a cutting board; remove foil. Cut into 9×½-inch slices using a serrated knife. Place slices, cut sides down, 1 inch apart on an ungreased cookie sheet. Bake 20 minutes or until crisp, turning carefully halfway through baking time. Cool completely on cookie sheet on a wire rack. Trim ends, if desired.

5. If desired, microwave chopped chocolate and 1 tablespoon shortening in a small microwave-safe bowl on medium 2 to 3 minutes or until melted and smooth, stirring twice. Brush or spread one end of each cookie stick with melted chocolate mixture; let excess drip down sides of cookie. Place cookies on parchment paper or waxed paper; let stand 1 hour or until set. Makes 18 cookies.

PER COOKIE *204 cal., 11 fat (5 g sat. fat), 18 mg chol., 44 mg sodium, 26 g carb., 1 g fiber 17 g sugars, 2 g pro.*

CHOCOLATE CHIP COOKIE DUNKERS

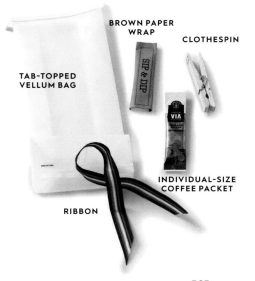

9-INCH ROUND FOIL PAN

RIBBON

11×¾-INCH SCRAPBOOKING PAPER STRIPS

TAB-TOPPED VELLUM BAG

BROWN PAPER WRAP

CLOTHESPIN

SIP & DIP

VIA

INDIVIDUAL-SIZE COFFEE PACKET

RIBBON

As a gift Place pan upside down and attach the ends of strips to the rim using crafts glue, gluing strips around the rim, overlapping each strip about ¼ inch (about 50 strips). Once dry, fold each strip around the rim of the tin. Insert cake in pan into pan. Gather strip ends, maintaining the overlap pattern, and center above pan, forming a chocolate "kiss" shape. Secure with a ribbon.

As a gift Arrange cookies in a vellum bag. Fold over top of bag and secure closed with the tabs. Enclose an individual-size coffee packet in a brown paper wrap. Attach the wrapped coffee packet and the ribbon to the top of the bag using a clothespin.

EASY MONSTER COOKIE BARS

½ cup semisweet chocolate pieces

½ cup chopped peanuts (optional)

1. Preheat oven to 350°F. Line a 9×9-inch baking pan with foil, extending foil over edges of pan. Lightly grease foil. Break up cookie dough into a large bowl. Stir in oats until combined. Stir in chocolate pieces and, if desired, nuts.

2. Pat mixture into prepared pan. Bake 20 minutes or until lightly browned. Cool in pan on a wire rack. Use the foil to lift uncut bars out of pan. Cut into bars. Makes 16 bars.

PER BAR *241 cal., 12 g fat (4 g sat. fat), 9 mg chol., 123 mg sodium, 31 g carb., 2 g fiber, 10 g sugars, 4 g pro.*

QUICK SEED BREAD

PREP 20 minutes

BAKE 45 minutes at 350°F

COOL 10 minutes

STAND 8 hours

1½ cups all-purpose flour

½ cup whole wheat flour

¾ cup packed brown sugar

½ cup dry roasted sunflower kernels

⅓ cup ground flax seeds

2 Tbsp. sesame seeds

2 Tbsp. poppy seeds

1 tsp. baking powder

½ tsp. baking soda

½ tsp. salt

1 egg

1¼ cups buttermilk or sour milk*

¼ cup vegetable oil

4 tsp. sesame seeds, poppy seeds, and/or dry-roasted sunflower kernels

1. Preheat oven to 350°F. Grease bottom and ½ inch up sides of a 9×5×3-inch loaf pan; set aside.

2. In a large bowl stir together the flours, brown sugar, ½ cup sunflower kernels, ground flax seed, the 2 tablespoons sesame seeds, the 2 tablespoons poppy seeds, the baking powder, baking soda, and salt. Make a well in center of flour mixture; set aside. In a medium bowl beat egg with a fork; stir in buttermilk and oil. Add egg mixture all at once to flour mixture. Stir just until moistened (batter should be lumpy). Spread batter into prepared pan. Sprinkle with 4 teaspoons seeds.

3. Bake 45 to 55 minutes or until a wooden toothpick inserted near center comes out clean. Cool in pan on a wire rack 10 minutes. Remove from pan. Cool completely on wire rack. Wrap and store bread 8 hours or overnight before slicing. Makes 14 servings.

***Tip** To make sour milk, place 4 teaspoons lemon juice or vinegar in a 2-cup glass measuring cup. Add enough milk to equal 1¼ cups; stir. Let stand 5 minutes before using.

PER SERVING *216 cal., 10 g fat (1 g sat. fat), 16 mg chol., 180 mg sodium, 28 g carb., 2 g fiber, 13 g sugars, 5 g pro.*

EASY MONSTER COOKIE BARS

PREP 15 minutes

BAKE 20 minutes at 350°F

1 16.5-oz. roll refrigerated peanut butter cookie dough

¾ cup rolled oats

1 cup candy-coated milk chocolate pieces

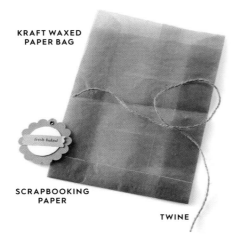

KRAFT WAXED PAPER BAG

SCRAPBOOKING PAPER

TWINE

As a gift Decorate a gift tag by attaching a white paper circle to a green scallop-edge circle using crafts glue. Attach a kraft paper tag across the center. Slide a bar cookie into a bag. Wrap wine around the bag to resemble a small package; tie on the tag.

As a gift Cut a rectangle opening on the front of the gift bag. Using glue stick, glue clear cellophane to the inside of the bag to cover the opening. Measure the opening; cut 4 strips of scrapbooking paper to that length. Cut one side of paper strips with scallop-edge scissors. Adhere strips with glue around window to form a border. Add a snowflake cutout to each corner. Tie a ribbon to bag handle.

SCRAPBOOKING PAPER

CELLOPHANE

PAPER BAG WITH HANDLES

RIBBON

SNOWFLAKE CUTOUTS

QUICK SEED BREAD

CHOCOLATE NUT FRUITCAKE

PREP 30 minutes
BAKE 1 hour 30 minutes at 300°F
COOL 10 minutes
STAND 8 hours

Nonstick cooking spray
1 cup candied red cherries, coarsely chopped
1 cup dried apricots, chopped
½ cup golden raisins
½ cup semisweet chocolate pieces
6 Tbsp. butter, softened
½ cup packed brown sugar
¼ cup granulated sugar
3 eggs
¼ cup orange juice
½ tsp. almond extract
1 cup all-purpose flour
½ tsp. baking powder
⅛ tsp. salt
1 cup walnuts, toasted and chopped (tip, page 105)
¾ cup pecans, toasted and chopped (tip, page 105)
¼ cup sliced almonds

1. Preheat oven to 300°F. Lightly coat a 9×5×3-inch loaf pan with nonstick cooking spray. Line bottom of pan with parchment or waxed paper; set aside. In bowl combine cherries, apricots, raisins, and chocolate; set aside.

2. In a large bowl beat butter and both sugars with a mixer on medium until light and fluffy. Beat in eggs, one at a time, until combined. Beat in orange juice and almond extract. Add flour, baking powder, and salt. Beat just until combined. Stir in fruit mixture, walnuts, and pecans. Spoon into prepared pan. Sprinkle with almonds.

3. Bake 1½ hours, or until wooden toothpick inserted near center comes out clean. Cool in pan on wire rack 10 minutes. Remove from pan; cool completely on rack. Wrap with plastic wrap and store 8 hours or overnight before serving. Makes 16 servings.

PER SERVING *311 cal., 16 g fat (5 g sat. fat), 51 mg chol., 78 mg sodium, 41 g carb., 3 g fiber, 21 g sugars, 5 g pro.*

As a gift Decorate a box using paints or markers. Wrap fruitcake with plastic wrap. Place loaf in the box and close top. Tie a string around the box.

CHOCOLATE NUT FRUITCAKE

KRAFT PAPER GABLE BOX

COLORED STRING

SWEET CURRIED PARTY NUTS

PREP 15 minutes
BAKE 40 minutes at 300°F

3½ cups bite-size pretzel twists
1   12-oz. container cocktail peanuts
1¼ cups whole almonds
1   cup roasted, salted pistachio nuts
1   cup shelled pumpkin seeds
    (pepitas) (optional)
½   cup light-color corn syrup
6   Tbsp. butter
⅓   cup packed brown sugar
2   Tbsp. curry powder
¼   tsp. salt
¼   tsp. cayenne pepper

1. Preheat oven to 300°F. Line an extra-large baking sheet or 2 large baking sheets with foil.
2. In a large roasting pan stir together the first four ingredients (through pistachios) and pumpkin seeds, if using.
3. In a small saucepan combine the remaining ingredients. Stir over medium heat until butter is melted and sugar is dissolved. Pour syrup over nut mixture; toss to coat.
4. Bake 40 to 45 minutes or until mixture is golden, stirring once or twice. Spread on prepared sheet(s). To cool, break snack mix apart. Spoon into gift bags; seal. Makes 10 servings.
PER SERVING *281 cal., 20 g fat (4 g sat. fat), 9 mg chol., 235 mg sodium, 19 g carb., 3 g fiber, 6 g sugars, 8 g pro.*

As a gift Reuse a pasta box by carefully undoing all glued flaps until flat. Refold the box with the printed portion on the inside; reglue the box. Wrap scrapbooking paper around the center of the box and adhere using crafts glue. Cut out a window in the paper to reveal the window in the box. Wrap ribbons around the top and bottom of paper band and attach ends using glue. Wrap a wider ribbon vertically around the box, attaching each end with a sticker tag.

SWEET CURRIED
PARTY NUTS

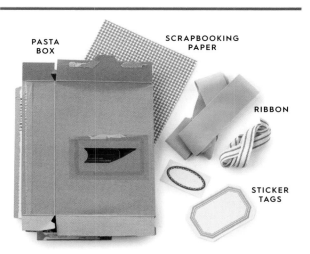

PASTA BOX

SCRAPBOOKING PAPER

RIBBON

STICKER TAGS

ALMOND SPRITZ

PREP 30 minutes
BAKE 8 minutes per batch at 350°F

1   cup butter, softened
1   3-oz. pkg. cream cheese, softened
1   cup sugar
¼   tsp. salt
1   egg yolk
1   tsp. vanilla
¼   tsp. almond extract
2½ cups all-purpose flour
     Colored sugars and/or small
     decorative candies (optional)
     Vanilla Icing (optional)

1. Preheat oven to 350°F. In a large bowl combine butter and cream cheese. Beat with a mixer on medium to high 30 seconds. Add sugar and salt. Beat until combined, scraping bowl occasionally. Add egg yolk, vanilla, and almond extract. Beat until combined. Beat in as much flour as you can with the mixer. Stir in any remaining flour.
2. Force unchilled dough through a cookie press fitted with your choice of design. Press dough 2 inches apart onto ungreased cookie sheets. If desired, sprinkle with colored sugar. Bake 8 to 10 minutes or until edges are firm but not browned. Remove cookies; cool on wire racks. If desired, brush or drizzle cookies with icing and decorate with colored sugars or candies. Makes 90 cookies.
Vanilla Icing In a small bowl stir together 1 cup powdered sugar, 1 tablespoon milk, and 1 teaspoon vanilla. If necessary, stir in additional milk to reach drizzling consistency.
PER COOKIE 44 cal., 2 fat (s g sat. fat), 8 mg chol., 26 mg sodium, 5 g carb., 0 g fiber, 2 g sugars, 0 g pro.

OATMEAL PEANUT BUTTER CUP COOKIES

PREP 20 minutes

1¼ cups rolled oats
¾   cup all-purpose flour
½   cup packed brown sugar
¼   cup granulated sugar
½   tsp. baking powder
⅛   tsp. baking soda
½   cup coarsely chopped dry-roasted
     peanuts
1   cup miniature chocolate-covered
     peanut butter cups, halved

1. In a 1-quart jar layer oats, flour, brown sugar, granulated sugar, baking powder, baking soda, and peanuts. Place peanut butter cups in a plastic bag. Set on top of peanuts in jar. Seal jar; include directions for making cookies.
TO MAKE COOKIES Preheat oven to 350°F. Line a cookie sheet with parchment paper or foil. Remove peanut butter cups from jar; set aside. Empty the remaining contents of the jar into a large bowl. In another bowl whisk together ½ cup creamy peanut butter, ¼ cup softened butter, 2 eggs, and ½ teaspoon vanilla. Add to flour mixture; stir until combined. Gently stir in peanut butter cups. Use a ¼-cup measure or scoop to drop mounds of dough about 4 inches apart onto prepared cookie sheet. Flatten dough mounds to about ¾ inch thick. Bake 12 to 14 minutes or until edges are brown. Cool on cookie sheet 1 minute. Remove cookies; cool on wire racks. (For regular-size cookies, drop dough by rounded teaspoons 2 inches apart on cookie sheet. Bake 9 to 11 minutes.) Makes 12 monster cookies or 36 regular cookies.
PER COOKIE 364 cal., 19 g fat (6 g sat. fat), 45 mg chol., 210 mg sodium, 41 g carb., 3 g fiber, 22 g sugars, 10 g pro.

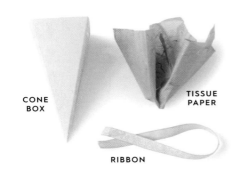

CONE BOX

TISSUE PAPER

RIBBON

As a gift Attach a paper flower from a crafts store to the top flap of the box lid using crafts glue or a decorative brad. Punch holes on opposite sides near the top of the box. Thread ribbon through the holes and tie ends together. Line box with tissue paper and fill with spritz cookies. Close box.

QUART JAR WITH DISK AND BAND LID

RECIPE CARD

FELT

RIBBON

As a gift Trace the disk lid on a piece of felt and cut out the circle. Fill the jar with cookie mix. Place the disk lid on top of jar, then place the felt circle on top. Secure the band lid around felt and disk. Write a recipe card with directions for mixing and baking. Wrap the recipe card around the jar and secure it with a ribbon. Glue ends of ribbon together with fabric glue.

OATMEAL PEANUT BUTTER CUP COOKIES

Recipe

Oatmeal Pea
— cup c
FROM THE

INGREDIENTS

1¼ c. rolled oats
¾ c. all-purpose flour
½ c. packed brown sugar
¼ c. granulated sugar
½ t. baking powder
⅛ t. baking soda

RED VELVET
SHORTBREAD
COOKIES

RED VELVET SHORTBREAD COOKIES

PREP 30 minutes
BAKE 20 minutes at 325°F

1¼   cups all-purpose flour
⅓   cup sugar
2   Tbsp. unsweetened cocoa powder
¼   tsp. salt
½   cup butter, cut up
1   Tbsp. red food coloring
3   oz. white chocolate (with cocoa butter), coarsely chopped
1½   tsp. shortening
    Finely chopped pistachios or white nonpareils (optional)

1. Preheat oven to 325°F. In a food processor combine flour, sugar, cocoa powder, and salt. Cover and pulse until combined. Add butter and red food coloring. Pulse until mixture resembles fine crumbs. Process just until mixture forms a ball.*
2. On a lightly floured surface, knead dough lightly until nearly smooth. Roll or pat dough to a ½-inch thickness. Using a floured 1½-inch round cutter, cut out dough. Place cutouts 1 inch apart on an ungreased cookie sheet. Press scraps together and reroll.
3. Bake 20 to 25 minutes or until centers are set. Remove cookies; cool on wire rack.
4. In a small heavy saucepan melt white chocolate and shortening over low heat, stirring constantly. Dip half of each cookie into melted chocolate. If desired, roll edges in pistachios or nonpareils. Let stand on waxed paper until set. Makes 24 cookies.
*Hand-mixing method In a medium bowl stir together flour, sugar, cocoa powder, and salt. Using a pastry blender, cut in butter and food coloring until mixture resembles fine crumbs and starts to cling together. Form mixture into a ball, kneading until smooth.
PER COOKIE *80 cal., 5 fat (3 g sat. fat), 9 mg chol., 47 mg sodium, 9 g carb., 0 g fiber, 4 g sugars, 1 g pro.*

SPICED PUMPKIN SNAPS DOG TREATS

PREP 30 minutes
BAKE 45 minutes at 300°F
STAND 8 hours

1	cup natural apple juice
1	cup canned pumpkin
¼	cup honey
2	Tbsp. canola oil
1¼	cups rolled oats
⅓	cup wheat germ
1	cup whole wheat flour
1	tsp. ground cinnamon
1½	cups all-purpose flour

1. Preheat oven to 300°F. Line two cookie sheets with parchment paper; set aside.
2. In a large saucepan heat and stir apple juice, pumpkin, honey, and oil until mixture simmers. Remove from heat. Stir in oats and wheat germ. Allow mixture to cool slightly. Stir in whole wheat flour and cinnamon. Stir in the all-purpose flour. Divide dough in half.

3. On a lightly floured surface, roll half the dough at a time to a 10-inch square. Using a pastry wheel or knife, cut dough into 2-inch squares. Place squares close together on prepared cookie sheets.
4. Bake on separate oven racks for 45 minutes, rotating sheets halfway through baking. Turn oven off; let dry in oven overnight. Transfer treats to two 1-quart canning jars. Store in the refrigerator. Makes 50 treats.
PER TREAT *48 cal., 1 g fat (0 g sat. fat), 0 mg chol., 1 mg sodium, 9 g carb., 1 g fiber, 2 g sugars, 1 g pro.*

SPICED PUMPKIN SNAPS DOG TREATS

GLASS REFRIGERATOR DISH

SCRAPBOOKING PAPER

STRING

DIE-CUT SCRAPBOOKING PAPER

As a gift Arrange cookies inside the glass dish; cover with the lid. Cut a strip of paper to wrap lengthwise around the dish, attaching ends together under dish using crafts glue. Use a die-cutting tool to make the button and scalloped tags, or purchase round tags and punch four holes in the center, as shown, using a paper punch. Using colored string, stitch an X through the four holes. Center the "button" on the paper strip on the dish and attach it using crafts glue.

As a gift Trace the disk lid on scrapbooking paper and cut out circle. Fill the jar with treats. Place the disk lid on jar, then place the paper circle on top. Secure the band lid around paper and disk. Wrap the twine around lid and tuck end under to secure. Tie the ribbon around jar at base of lid. Wrap the paper strip around the jar and attach ends using crafts glue. Create label using white press-on letters and brads. Glue label to front of jar.

QUART JAR

3×12-INCH STRIP SCRAPBOOKING PAPER

TWINE

RIBBON

New Year's Eve Soirée

Ring in the new year with a festive feast for friends and family. Whether for a spread of appetizers and desserts or an elegant dinner, this collection of celebration-ready recipes welcomes the coming year in big style—and taste.

CHARCUTERIE
PLATTER, PAGE 132

PEPPERED ALMONDS

1. On a large platter arrange pate (if using), prosciutto, soppressata, mortadella, small piles of onions (if desired), cornichons, mixed olives, a small ramekin with mustard, baguette slices, and lemon wedges.
2. If not serving immediately, cover and refrigerate up to 2 hours. Let stand 30 minutes at room temperature before serving to bring out the fullest flavors. Makes 12 servings.

PER SERVING *627 cal., 39 g fat (15 g sat. fat), 98 mg chol., 2,209 mg sodium, 31 g carb., 2 g fiber, 7 g sugars, 27 g pro.*

JALAPEÑO POPPER DIP

PREP 20 minutes
SLOW COOK 2 hours (low)

1   8-oz. pkg. cream cheese, cut up
1   8-oz. carton sour cream
1   cup shredded cheddar cheese (4 oz.)
3   slices bacon, crisp-cooked and crumbled
2   to 3 fresh jalapeño chile peppers, seeded (if desired) and finely chopped*
1½ tsp. chili powder
2   cloves garlic, minced
1   tsp. butter
¼   cup panko bread crumbs
    Hot and/or sweet pepper strips
    Chili powder (optional)

1. In a 1½- or 2-quart slow cooker combine the first seven ingredients (through garlic). Cover and cook on low 2 hours, stirring once halfway through cooking.
2. Before serving, in a large skillet melt butter over medium heat. Stir in bread crumbs; cook 3 to 4 minutes or until brown, stirring occasionally. Sprinkle over dip. Serve with pepper strips. If desired, sprinkle dip with chili powder. Makes 10 servings.

*Tip Chile peppers contain oils that can irritate your skin and eyes. Wear plastic or rubber gloves when working with them.

PER SERVING *190 cal., 17 g fat (10 g sat. fat), 52 mg chol., 225 mg sodium, 3 g carb., 0 g fiber, 2 g sugars, 6 g pro.*

PEPPERED ALMONDS

START TO FINISH 30 minutes

2   cups whole raw almonds with skins
1   Tbsp. extra-virgin olive oil
1   Tbsp. cracked black pepper
1   tsp. kosher salt

1. Preheat oven to 350°F. In shallow baking pan combine almonds, oil, pepper, and salt. Roast 10 to 12 minutes or until almonds are toasted, shaking pan once. Remove; cool. Store in an airtight container at room temperature up to 2 weeks. Makes 8 servings.

PER SERVING *224 cal., 20 g fat (2 g sat. fat), 0 mg chol., 141 mg sodium, 8 g carb., 5 g fiber, 2 g sugars, 8 g pro.*

CHARCUTERIE PLATTER (PHOTO, PAGE 130)

PREP 30 minutes
STAND 30 minutes

1   3.2- to 4-oz. can mushroom and/or liver pate, chilled and thinly sliced (optional)
6   oz. prosciutto, thinly sliced
6   oz. soppressata, thinly sliced
6   oz. mortadella, thinly sliced
1   3.25- to 3.75-oz. jar cocktail onions, drained (optional)
¾   cup cornichons or sour gherkins
¾   cup marinated mixed olives
½   cup coarse Dijon mustard
1   fresh baguette, thinly sliced
    Lemon wedges

JALAPEÑO
POPPER DIP

CHICKEN
MEATBALLS WITH
SUN-DRIED
TOMATOES

CHICKEN MEATBALLS WITH SUN-DRIED TOMATOES

PREP 25 minutes
BAKE 16 minutes at 350°F

3½ oz. oil-packed dried tomatoes, well-drained (¾ cup)
3 cloves garlic
¼ tsp. kosher salt
⅛ tsp. freshly ground black pepper
¼ cup seasoned fine dry bread crumbs
1½ lb. ground chicken
½ cup whole milk ricotta cheese
2 eggs, lightly beaten
1 Tbsp. whole milk
1 Tbsp. chopped fresh parsley
2 tsp. dried thyme, crushed
1 tsp. dried oregano, crushed
1 tsp. dried marjoram, crushed
2 Tbsp. olive oil
1 recipe White Sauce (optional)

1. Preheat the oven to 350°F.
2. In a food processor pulse the dried tomatoes, garlic, salt, and pepper. Add the bread crumbs and pulse to combine.
3. Transfer the mixture to a large bowl. Add chicken, ricotta cheese, eggs, milk, parsley, thyme, oregano, and marjoram. Combine until uniform in appearance. Roll into 1½-inch balls.
4. Line a 15×10×1-inch baking pan with parchment paper. Brush paper with olive oil. Place meatballs in pan. Bake 16 minutes or until cooked through (165°F). If desired, serve meatballs with White Sauce. Makes 8 servings.
PER SERVING *47 cal., 3 g fat (1 g sat. fat), 26 mg chol., 46 mg sodium, 1 g carb., 0 g fiber, 0 g sugars, 4 g pro.*
White Sauce In a medium saucepan combine 3 tablespoons all-purpose flour and 2 tablespoons butter over medium-high heat. Cook and stir 2 minutes or until very light golden brown. Add 1 cup chicken broth, 1 cup heavy cream, 1 tablespoon white balsamic vinegar, 1 teaspoon Worcestershire sauce, ½ teaspoon dried thyme, ¼ teaspoon salt, and ⅛ teaspoon black pepper. Cook and stir until thickened and bubbly. Cook and stir 1 minute more. Stir in 2 tablespoons chopped fresh Italian parsley.

ORANGE SHRIMP AND AVOCADO CROSTINI

PREP 15 minutes
BROIL 2 minutes
COOK 3 minutes

16 fresh or frozen large shrimp
1 orange
1 large ripe avocado, halved, seeded, and peeled
½ tsp. salt, divided
⅛ tsp. black pepper
2 tsp. snipped fresh Italian parsley
1 tsp. snipped fresh chives
16 ½-inch slices baguette-style French bread
2 Tbsp. olive oil
2 cloves garlic, minced
¼ tsp. crushed red pepper

1. Thaw shrimp, if frozen. Peel and devein shrimp. Rinse shrimp; pat dry with paper towels. Remove 1 teaspoon zest and 2 teaspoons juice from the orange.
2. Preheat broiler. In a bowl combine avocado, orange juice, ¼ teaspoon of the salt, and black pepper; mash gently. Stir in parsley and chives.
3. Arrange bread slices on a large baking sheet. Brush slices with 1 tablespoon olive oil. Broil 3 to 4 inches from heat 2 minutes or until toasted, turning once.
4. In a large nonstick skillet heat remaining 1 tablespoon olive oil over medium-high heat. Add shrimp, garlic, crushed red pepper, and remaining ¼ teaspoon salt. Cook and stir 3 minutes or until shrimp are opaque. Stir in orange zest.
5. Spread avocado mixture onto crostini. Top with shrimp. If desired, sprinkle with additional parsley and chives. Makes 16 servings.
PER SERVING *69 cal., 3 g fat (0 g sat. fat), 17 mg chol., 143 mg sodium, 6 g carb., 1 g fiber, 0 g sugars, 3 g pro.*

ORANGE SHRIMP AND AVOCADO CROSTINI

CAPONATA WITH
PITA CRISPS

CUBANA
COGNAC

CAPONATA WITH PITA CRISPS

PREP 12 minutes
ROAST 20 minutes at 450°F
STAND 10 minutes

1   medium eggplant, halved lengthwise
1   medium red sweet pepper, halved
1   medium red onion, cut into wedges
2   cloves garlic
     Olive oil nonstick cooking spray
2   medium roma tomatoes, chopped
2   Tbsp. red wine vinegar
2   tsp. capers, drained
1   tsp. honey
½   tsp. dried Italian seasoning, crushed
     Pita chips

1. Preheat oven to 450°F. Line a 9×13-inch baking pan with foil. Place the eggplant, cut sides up, on the baking sheet. Place sweet pepper halves, cut sides down, in baking pan. Place onion wedges and garlic in baking pan. Lightly coat vegetables with cooking spray. Roast, uncovered, 20 minutes or until vegetables are tender and sweet pepper skins are lightly charred. Place vegetables in a bowl; cover and let stand 10 minutes.

2. Remove and discard skins from eggplant and sweet pepper. Chop vegetables; place in a large bowl. Stir in remaining ingredients except pita chips. Serve with pita chips. Makes 6 servings.
PER SERVING *132 cal., 1 fat (0 g sat. fat), 0 mg chol., 204 mg sodium, 28 g carb., 7 g fiber, 6 g sugars, 5 g pro.*

CUBANA COGNAC

START TO FINISH 10 minutes

1   Tbsp. sugar
½   oz. lemon juice (1 Tbsp.)
½   oz. lime juice (1 Tbsp.)
6   to 8 fresh mint leaves
2   oz. Cognac or other brandy (¼ cup)
     Ice
⅓   to ½ cup club soda, chilled (optional)
     Lemon and/or lime wedges (optional)

1. In a highball glass combine sugar, lemon juice, and lime juice, stirring to dissolve sugar. Add mint. To muddle, gently crush mint with the back of a spoon. Add Cognac. Fill the highball glass with ice. If desired, slowly pour in club soda; stir gently to combine. If desired, add lemon and/or lime wedges. Makes 1 serving.
PER SERVING *205 cal., 0 fat, 0 mg chol., 2 mg sodium, 15 g carb., 0 g fiber, 13 g sugars, 0 g pro.*

MINTED GRAPEFRUIT PUNCH

START TO FINISH 20 minutes

½   cup loosely packed fresh mint leaves
2   Tbsp. organic cane sugar
6   cups freshly squeezed grapefruit juice or refrigerated grapefruit juice
3   cups vodka
     Crushed ice
     Club soda, chilled
     Grapefruit slices

1. Muddle mint leaves and cane sugar together in a sturdy pitcher. Add grapefruit juice and vodka; stir to mix. Serve over crushed ice with a splash of club soda and grapefruit slices. Makes 12 servings.
PER SERVING *195 cal., 0 fat, 0 mg chol., 7 mg sodium, 16 g carb., 1 g fiber, 13 g sugars, 1 g pro.*

MINTED
GRAPEFRUIT
PUNCH

TWICE-BAKED
CRÈME FRAÎCHE
POTATOES

BRAISED BEEF SHANKS WITH MUSHROOMS AND OLIVES

PREP 35 minutes
ROAST 2 hours at 325°F

- 2 Tbsp. olive oil
- 4 lb. beef shank crosscuts, cut 1¼ inches thick
   Salt and black pepper
- 2 cups chopped onions
- 1 cup coarsely chopped carrots
- 3 cloves garlic, minced
- ¾ cup dry red wine or beef broth
- 1 14.5-oz. can diced tomatoes with basil, garlic, and oregano, undrained
- 1 cup beef broth
- 12 oz. fresh cremini or button mushrooms, quartered or halved
- ¾ cup assorted pitted olives
- ¼ cup snipped fresh Italian parsley
- 2 tsp. lemon zest
- 3 cloves garlic, minced
   Hot cooked gnocchi (optional)

1. Preheat oven to 325°F. In a Dutch oven heat oil over medium-high heat. Add beef shanks; cook until browned on all sides. Remove shanks; sprinkle with salt and pepper.
2. Add onions, carrots, and garlic to Dutch oven. Cook 5 minutes or until tender, stirring occasionally. Carefully add wine, stirring to scrape up any crusty brown bits. Add tomatoes and broth; return beef shanks to Dutch oven. Bring to boiling. Cover pot and transfer to oven.
3. Roast 2 to 3 hours or until shanks are tender, adding mushrooms the last 20 minutes of roasting. Transfer shanks to a platter.
4. Strain vegetables from cooking liquid. Stir olives into vegetables and spoon over beef shanks. Skim fat from cooking liquid. Drizzle liquid over shanks, vegetables, and, if desired, gnocchi. In a small bowl combine parsley, lemon zest, and garlic; sprinkle over servings. Makes 8 servings.
PER SERVING *387 cal., 20 g fat (6 g sat. fat), 66 mg chol., 666 mg sodium, 13 g carb., 2 g fiber, 6 g sugars, 34 g pro.*

BRAISED BEEF SHANKS WITH MUSHROOMS AND OLIVES

TWICE-BAKED CRÈME FRAÎCHE POTATOES

PREP 20 minutes
BAKE 1 hour 15 minutes at 375°F
COOL 10 minutes

- 8 6- to 8-oz. russet potatoes
- 2 tsp. vegetable oil
- 1 8-oz. container crème fraîche
- ½ cup chopped mixed fresh herbs, such as chives, sage, thyme, savory, and/or marjoram
- ¼ cup half-and-half
- 3 Tbsp. unsalted butter, softened
   Kosher salt and black pepper

1. Position rack in center of oven; preheat to 375°F. Line a baking sheet with foil. Pierce potatoes in several spots with a fork. Rub oil over potatoes. Place directly on center oven rack. Place foil-lined baking sheet on rack below potatoes. Bake 45 minutes or until very tender. Transfer to a wire rack; cool 10 minutes. Use oven mitts to hold each hot potato. With a serrated knife cut off top quarter of potato. Using a spoon, scoop out flesh, leaving ¼-inch-thick shells; transfer flesh to a large bowl. Mash potato in bowl until smooth. Mix in crème fraîche, herbs, half-and-half, and butter. Season with kosher salt and pepper.
2. Spoon or pipe mashed potato into prepared shells. Place on a 15×10-inch baking pan. Bake 30 minutes or until heated through. Makes 8 servings.
Make-Ahead Potatoes can be made through Step 2; cover loosely with plastic wrap, and chill up to 24 hours. Bake filled potatoes at 375°F for 45 minutes or until filling is heated through and top is lightly browned.
PER SERVING *303 cal., 17 g fat (10 g sat. fat), 39 mg chol., 21 mg sodium, 31 g carb., 2 g fiber, 1 g sugars, 4 g pro.*

ROASTED ROOT VEGETABLE AND ROMAINE SALAD

PREP 15 minutes
ROAST 30 minutes at 375°F
COOL 15 minutes

1½ lb. carrots, turnips, and/or parsnips
2 small shallots, peeled and quartered
3 Tbsp. olive oil
¼ tsp. salt
  Black pepper
1 medium pear, cored and coarsely chopped
2 Tbsp. white wine vinegar
1½ tsp. snipped fresh thyme
½ tsp. Dijon mustard
½ tsp. honey
1 clove garlic, minced
4 cups torn romaine lettuce
¼ cup coarsely chopped pecans, toasted (tip, page 105)
1 Tbsp. coarsely chopped fresh Italian parsley

1. Preheat oven to 375°F. Peel carrots and bias-cut into 1-inch pieces. Place in a 13×9-inch baking pan. Add shallots. Toss with 1 Tbsp. of the olive oil. Sprinkle with ⅛ tsp. of the salt and pepper to taste.
2. Roast, uncovered, 15 minutes. Stir in pear. Roast about 15 minutes more or until vegetables are tender. Cool slightly.
3. Meanwhile, for dressing, in a screw-top jar combine the remaining 2 Tbsp. olive oil, ⅛ teaspoon of the salt and the next five ingredients (through garlic); add pepper to taste. Cover and shake well.
4. In a bowl combine lettuce and dressing; toss to coat. Transfer to a platter. Top with roasted vegetables and pear. Sprinkle with pecans and parsley. Makes 6 servings.
PER SERVING *168 cal., 10 g fat (1 g sat. fat), 0 mg chol., 189 mg sodium, 19 g carb., 5 g fiber, 10 g sugars, 2 g pro.*

HARVEST WILD RICE SALAD

PREP 30 minutes
COOK 45 minutes
CHILL 1 hour

1½ cups uncooked wild rice, rinsed and drained
4 cups water
2 tsp. kosher salt
1 recipe Citrus Vinaigrette
4 navel oranges, peeled, sectioned, and cut into 1-inch pieces (1 cup)
2 stalks celery, bias-sliced ¼-inch thick
1 red apple, cored and coarsely chopped
1 pear, cored and coarsely chopped
1 cup coarsely chopped roasted, salted pistachios
2 cups watercress

1. Place rice, water, and salt in a large saucepan. Bring to boiling; reduce heat. Cover and simmer 45 to 50 minutes or until rice is tender. Drain well and cool. In a large bowl mix together the Citrus Vinaigrette. Add wild rice. Cover and chill 1 hour or up to 24 hours.
2. To serve, add oranges, celery, apple, pear, and pistachios to wild rice mixture; stir to coat. Add watercress and toss gently. Makes 22 servings.
Citrus Vinaigrette Remove 1 teaspoon zest and ⅓ cup juice from 1 orange. In a screw-top jar combine orange juice and zest, ¼ cup cider vinegar, 2 tablespoons finely chopped shallot, 1 tablespoon honey, 1 teaspoon Dijon mustard, ⅛ teaspoon salt, and ¼ cup extra-virgin olive oil. Cover and shake well.
PER SERVING *120 cal., 5 g fat (1 g sat. fat), 0 mg chol., 190 mg sodium, 16 g carb., 2 g fiber, 6 g sugars, 3 g pro.*

ROASTED ROOT VEGETABLE AND ROMAINE SALAD

FEATHER ROLLS

FEATHER ROLLS

PREP 40 minutes
CHILL 2 hours
REST 10 minutes
RISE 40 minutes
BAKE 12 minutes at 375°F

4¼ to 4¾ cups all-purpose flour
1   pkg. active dry yeast
1½ cups warm water (120°F to 130°F)
½   cup mashed cooked potato
⅓   cup butter, melted
¼   cup sugar
1¼ tsp. salt
2   Tbsp. butter, melted

1. In a large bowl combine 2 cups of the flour and the yeast. In a medium bowl combine the warm water, mashed potato, the ⅓ cup melted butter, sugar, and salt. Add potato mixture to flour mixture. Beat with a mixer on low 30 seconds, scraping sides of bowl constantly. Beat on high 3 minutes, scraping sides of bowl occasionally. Stir in as much of the remaining flour as you can.
2. Turn dough out onto a lightly floured surface. Knead in enough of the remaining flour to make a moderately soft dough that is smooth and elastic (3 to 5 minutes total). Place dough in a greased bowl, turning once to grease the surface. Cover; chill 2 hours.
3. Punch dough down. Divide in half. Cover and let rest 10 minutes. Meanwhile, lightly grease two baking sheets. On a lightly floured surface, roll each dough half into a 12-inch circle. Brush with 1 tablespoon of the melted butter. Cut each circle into 8 wedges. To shape rolls, begin at wide end of each wedge and loosely roll toward the point. Place, point sides down, 2 to 3 inches apart on prepared baking sheets. Cover and let rise in a warm place until nearly double in size (about 40 minutes).
4. Preheat oven to 375°F. Bake 12 to 15 minutes or until rolls are golden and sound hollow when lightly tapped. Immediately remove from pan. Serve warm. Makes 16 rolls.
PER ROLL *198 cal., 6 g fat (4 g sat. fat), 15 mg chol., 245 mg sodium, 32 g carb., 1 g fiber, 4 g sugars, 4 g pro.*

CARROT CAKE WITH
CREAM CHEESE
MASCARPONE
FROSTING

CARROT CAKE WITH CREAM CHEESE MASCARPONE FROSTING

PREP 45 minutes
BAKE 30 minutes at 350°F
COOL 10 minutes

4   large carrots, peeled
2½   cups all-purpose flour
2   tsp. ground cinnamon
1   tsp. baking soda
½   tsp. salt
½   tsp. ground cardamom
¼   tsp. freshly grated nutmeg
1   cup unsalted butter, at room temperature
2   cups sugar
1   tsp. vanilla
5   eggs, separated, at room temperature
¾   cup buttermilk
1   recipe Mascarpone Frosting
      Carrot curls (optional)

1. Preheat oven to 350°F. Grease and flour two 9-inch round baking pans and line with parchment paper; set aside. Finely shred 3 of the carrots and coarsely shred 1 carrot. In a medium bowl whisk together the next six ingredients (through nutmeg).
2. In a large bowl beat the butter with a mixer on medium 30 seconds. Gradually beat in sugar until combined, scraping sides of bowl occasionally. Beat in the carrots and vanilla until combined. Beat in egg yolks, one at a time, beating just until combined after each addition. Alternately add flour mixture and buttermilk to butter mixture (batter will be thick).
3. Thoroughly wash beaters. In a large clean bowl beat egg whites with a mixer just until stiff peaks form (tips stand straight). Fold into butter mixture. Divide between prepared pans, filling each with about 3 cups batter (about one-third full). Bake 30 minutes or until cakes pull away from sides of pans and a toothpick inserted near centers comes out clean. Cool in pans on wire racks 10 minutes. Remove from pans and cool completely on wire racks. Spread with Mascarpone Frosting. If desired, top with carrot curls. Makes 16 servings.
Mascarpone Frosting In an extra-large bowl beat 1½ cups (3 sticks) softened unsalted butter, one 8-ounce package softened cream cheese, and one 8-ounce container softened mascarpone cheese until combined. Add ¼ teaspoon kosher salt, ¼ teaspoon ground cardamon, and 1 teaspoon vanilla. Gradually add 1 pound powdered sugar, beating just until smooth.
PER SERVING 682 cal., 42 g fat (25 g sat. fat), 171 mg chol., 292 mg sodium, 72 g carb., 1 g fiber, 55 g sugars, 6 g pro.

MILK CHOCOLATE BROWNIES

PREP 25 minutes
BAKE 25 minutes at 325°F

      Nonstick cooking spray
⅔   cup all-purpose flour
½   tsp. baking powder
½   tsp. salt
½   cup butter
1   cup milk chocolate pieces
3   oz. unsweetened chocolate, chopped
1   cup sugar
1½   tsp. vanilla
3   eggs
1   recipe Caramel Frosting
¼   cup milk chocolate pieces, melted

1. Preheat oven to 325°F. Line a 9-inch square baking pan with foil, extending the foil over edges of pan. Coat foil with cooking spray. In a bowl stir together flour, baking powder, and salt.
2. In a medium saucepan heat and stir butter, ½ cup of the milk chocolate pieces, and the unsweetened chocolate over low heat until melted and smooth. Cool slightly. Stir in sugar and vanilla until combined. Add eggs, one at a time, beating with a wooden spoon after each addition. Stir in flour mixture just until combined. Stir in remaining ½ cup milk chocolate pieces. Pour batter into the prepared baking pan. Bake 25 minutes. Cool in pan on a wire rack.
3. Spread brownies with Caramel Frosting. Fill a small heavy resealable plastic bag with the melted chocolate. Snip off a small corner. Pipe chocolate in diagonal lines across the brownies. Give pan a one-quarter turn. Pipe remaining chocolate in diagonal lines across brownies to form a crosshatch pattern. Chill until set. Using the edges of the foil, lift uncut brownies out of pan. Transfer to a cutting board. Cut into bars. Makes 20 bars.
Caramel Frosting In a large bowl beat ⅓ cup butter, softened, with a mixer on medium until smooth. Gradually add 1 cup powdered sugar, beating well. Slowly beat in ¼ cup caramel ice cream topping and ⅛ teaspoon. salt. Gradually beat in an additional 2 cups powdered sugar. Beat in 2 to 3 tablespoons milk to spreading consistency.
PER BAR 314 cal., 15 g fat (10 g sat. fat), 53 mg chol., 180 mg sodium, 45 g carb., 2 g fiber, 38 g sugars, 3 g pro.

MILK CHOCOLATE BROWNIES

CHOCOLATE CHUNK AND
CARAMEL PECAN PIE,
PAGE 154

TOASTED COUSCOUS
AND CHARD SALAD,
PAGE 150

Weekend Guests

When holiday houseguests arrive, be prepared with easygoing
meals. These dishes offer time to relax and enjoy the pleasure
of your company.

BARBECUE
SNACK MIX

BARBECUE SNACK MIX

PREP 10 minutes
SLOW COOK 2 hours (low) or 1 hour (high)
COOL 30 minutes

    Nonstick cooking spray
3   cups crispy corn and rice cereal
2   cups bite-size multibran cereal
2   cups oyster crackers
⅔   cup slivered almonds
1   tsp. dried thyme leaves, crushed
1   tsp. paprika
1   tsp. packed brown sugar
¼   tsp. ground cumin
¼   tsp. dry mustard
⅛   tsp. cayenne pepper
3   Tbsp. olive oil

1. Lightly coat a 5- to 6-quart slow cooker with cooking spray. Add cereals, crackers, and almonds. In a small bowl combine thyme, paprika, brown sugar, cumin, mustard, and cayenne. Drizzle cereal mixture with oil, tossing to coat. Sprinkle with spice mixture, tossing to coat.

2. Cover and cook on low 2 hours, stirring every 30 minutes or on high 1 hour, stirring every 20 minutes.

3. Spread snack mix in an even layer on a 9×13-inch baking pan; cool completely. Makes 24 servings.

PER SERVING *81 cal., 4 g fat (0 g sat. fat), 0 mg chol., 115 mg sodium, 12 g carb., 1 g fiber, 2 g sugars, 1 g pro.*

FRENCH-FRIED ONION DIP

PREP 25 minutes
SLOW COOK 2 hours (low) or 1 hour (high)

1   16-oz. carton sour cream
½   8-oz. pkg. reduced-fat cream cheese (neufchatel), cubed
⅔   cup light mayonnaise
½   cup finely shredded Parmesan cheese (2 oz.)
½   cup thinly sliced green onions
2   Tbsp. all-purpose flour
1   2.8-oz. can French-fried onions
    Milk (optional)

    Baguette-style French bread slices, toasted

1. In a 1½- or 2-quart slow cooker combine the first six ingredients (through flour). Reserve 2 tablespoons of the French-fried onions for topping. Stir the remaining onions into cheese mixture.

2. Cover and cook on low 2 to 3 hours or on high 1 to 1½ hours. Before serving, whisk until smooth, adding milk if needed to reach desired consistency.

3. Serve immediately or keep warm, covered, on warm or low up to 2 hours. Sprinkle with the reserved French-fried onions and additional green onions. Serve with bread slices. Makes 26 servings.

PER SERVING *91 cal., 8 g fat (4 g sat. fat), 15 mg chol., 137 mg sodium, 3 g carb., 0 g fiber, 1 g sugars, 2 g pro.*

FRENCH-FRIED ONION DIP

SPINACH AND FETA TART

2 tablespoons oil. Season to taste with additional salt and pepper. Top tart with sauteed lemons. Serve with tossed spinach and additional feta, if desired. Makes 6 servings.

PER SERVING *469 cal., 36 g fat (14 g sat. fat), 98 mg chol., 578 mg sodium, 24 g carb., 3 g fiber, 2 g sugars, 10 g pro.*

CREAM OF CARROT SOUP

PREP 40 minutes
COOK 40 minutes

8	oz. thick-sliced bacon (about 6 slices), chopped
¼	cup fresh sage leaves
2	lb. carrots, peeled and chopped
2	large onions, sliced
6	cloves garlic, minced
½	tsp. kosher salt
1	7- to 8-oz. russet potato, peeled and chopped (1⅓ cups)
6	cups reduced-sodium chicken broth
⅓	cup heavy cream
	Crumbled blue cheese
	Black pepper

1. Cook bacon in a 5- to 6-quart Dutch oven until browned and crisp; remove and drain on paper towels, reserving drippings. Add sage leaves to hot drippings and cook 1 to 2 minutes or until sage leaves no longer sizzle; remove and drain with bacon. Remove all but 1 tablespoon of bacon drippings from the pot. Cook carrots, onions, garlic, and salt in reserved drippings 10 minutes, stirring occasionally, until onion is tender. Add potato and broth to pot. Bring to boiling, reduce heat, and simmer, covered, 40 minutes or until potatoes and carrots are very tender.
2. Puree soup until smooth with an immersion blender*; add cream and heat through. Top soup with reserved bacon, sage leaves, blue cheese, and cracked black pepper. Makes 6 servings.
*Tip If you do not have an immersion blender, use a food processor or blender and puree soup in small batches, returning to pot to heat through.
PER SERVING *245 cal., 11 g fat (5 g sat. fat), 31 mg chol., 1,017 mg sodium, 28 g carb., 6 g fiber, 10 g sugars, 10 g pro.*

SPINACH AND FETA TART

PREP 30 minutes
BAKE 30 minutes at 400°F
CHILL 15 minutes

2	lemons
	Kosher salt and black pepper
4	Tbsp. extra-virgin olive oil
6	green onions, thinly sliced
1	lb. fresh spinach, tough stems removed
½	17.3-oz. pkg. frozen puff pastry sheets (1 sheet), thawed
2	eggs
½	cup crème fraîche
2	Tbsp. snipped fresh dill
½	tsp. kosher salt
¼	tsp. black pepper
⅛	tsp. freshly grated nutmeg
4	oz. feta cheese, crumbled
½	cup fresh mint leaves, torn if large
¼	cup fresh dill sprigs

1. For the sauteed lemons, thinly slice 1 lemon. Season with salt and pepper. In a large skillet heat 1 tablespoon olive oil over medium heat. Cook slices 3 to 5 minutes or until browned, turning once. Remove from heat. Let cool.
2. In an extra-large skillet heat 1 tablespoon oil over medium-high heat. Add the green onions; cook and stir 2 minutes or until tender and fragrant.
3. Gradually add about 12 cups of the spinach, tossing with tongs until wilted, about 2 minutes. Remove and cool slightly. Drain and squeeze spinach mixture to remove as much liquid as possible. Coarsely chop the spinach.
4. Preheat oven to 400°F. Line a baking sheet with parchment paper. On a lightly floured surface, roll out puff pastry sheet to a 13×11-inch rectangle. Carefully transfer pastry to the prepared sheet. Moisten edges of pastry with water and fold over ½-inch borders on all sides; press borders lightly. Using the back of a paring knife, make evenly spaced indentations around the edge of pastry (to help the border rise evenly). Chill pastry 15 minutes or up to 1 hour.
5. Meanwhile, remove 1 teaspoon zest and 1 tablespoon juice from remaining lemon. In a medium bowl whisk together lemon zest, eggs, crème fraîche, snipped dill, salt, pepper, and nutmeg. Stir in chopped spinach and feta. Spread on pastry. Bake 30 minutes or until pastry is puffed and browned on the bottom and filling is set. Slide tart onto a wire rack to cool.
6. Just before serving, toss remaining spinach, mint leaves, and dill sprigs with the lemon juice and remaining

CREAM OF
CARROT SOUP

ROASTED SWEET POTATOES WITH GREENS

ROASTED SWEET POTATOES WITH GREENS

PREP 10 minutes
ROAST 34 minutes at 450°F

3	to 4 lb. sweet potatoes, halved lengthwise and cut into wedges
2	Tbsp. olive oil
1	tsp. salt
½	tsp. black pepper
½	cup chopped hazelnuts
4	cloves garlic, minced
2	cups arugula
½	cup cider vinegar

1. Preheat oven to 450°F. Place potatoes in a 15×10-inch baking pan. Drizzle with oil and sprinkle with salt and pepper; toss to coat.
2. Roast 30 minutes or until tender, turning once. Sprinkle with hazelnuts and garlic. Roast 4 to 5 minutes more or until nuts are toasted. Top with arugula and drizzle with vinegar. Makes 8 servings.
PER SERVING *236 cal., 9 g fat (1 g sat. fat), 0 mg chol., 387 mg sodium, 37 g carb., 6 g fiber, 8 g sugars, 4 g pro.*

TOASTED COUSCOUS AND CHARD SALAD

(PHOTO, PAGE 145)

START TO FINISH 20 minutes

1	14.5-oz. can reduced-sodium chicken broth
2	Tbsp. butter
1	tsp. Aleppo pepper
½	tsp. kosher salt
¼	tsp. freshly ground black pepper
1	bunch green onions, trimmed and finely chopped
1	cup Israeli couscous (large pearl)
1	cup shredded raw golden beets*
1	cup lightly packed fresh Italian parsley
½	cup pomegranate seeds
⅓	cup chopped toasted walnuts (tip, page 67)
¼	cup mint leaves
2	Tbsp. red wine vinegar
1	Tbsp. pomegranate molasses
8	oz. rainbow chard, stemmed and thinly sliced
2	Tbsp. extra-virgin olive oil

1. In a small saucepan bring chicken broth to boiling. Reduce heat to low, cover, and keep warm.

TORTELLINI
WITH
BROCCOLINI

2. Meanwhile, in an extra-large nonstick skillet melt butter with Aleppo pepper, salt, and ground black pepper over medium-high heat. Add green onions and cook about 1 minute or until fragrant. Add couscous and cook 5 minutes or until toasted. Slowly stir in broth then bring to boiling. Reduce heat and cook, uncovered, 10 minutes or until couscous is tender and liquid has been absorbed, stirring occasionally. Stir in beets; heat through.

3. Remove skillet from heat and add the parsley, pomegranate seeds, walnuts, ¼ cup mint, vinegar, and molasses; toss gently to combine. Toss with chard and drizzle with olive oil before serving. Top with additional mint. Makes 8 servings.

*Shred the beets when you are ready to cook. They will discolor if allowed to stand.

PER SERVING *189 cal., 8 g fat (2 g sat. fat), 8 mg chol., 293 mg sodium, 25 g carb., 2 g fiber, 5 g sugars, 5 g pro.*

TORTELLINI WITH BROCCOLI

START TO FINISH 25 minutes

9 oz. refrigerated three-cheese-filled tortellini
2 cups broccoli florets, or 8 oz. broccolini, cut up
1 15- to 19-oz. can cannellini (white kidney beans), rinsed and drained
¼ cup slivered pitted Kalamata olives
2 Tbsp. olive oil
2 Tbsp. white balsamic vinegar
½ tsp. crushed red pepper
1 cup quartered cherry or grape tomatoes
½ cup crumbled feta cheese (2 oz.)
¼ cup snipped fresh basil

1. In a large deep skillet bring 1 to 2 inches of water to boiling. Add tortellini; cook 7 to 8 minutes or until tender, stirring occasionally. Stir in broccoli; cook 1 to 2 minutes or until broccoli is crisp-tender. Drain in colander. Return tortellini and broccoli to skillet.

2. Stir the next five ingredients (through crushed red pepper) into pasta mixture. Heat through. Top with tomatoes, cheese, and basil. Makes 4 servings.

PER SERVING *448 cal., 18 g fat (6 g sat. fat), 41 mg chol., 907 mg sodium, 53 g carb., 8 g fiber, 9 g sugars, 19 g pro.*

CHEESEBURGER-
STYLE MEAT LOAF
SANDWICH

CHEESEBURGER-STYLE MEAT LOAF SANDWICH

PREP 25 minutes
BAKE 1 hour 10 minutes at 350°F
STAND 5 minutes
BROIL 4 minutes

⅓ cup fine dry bread crumbs
1 egg, lightly beaten
3 Tbsp. finely chopped onion
3 Tbsp. finely chopped dill pickle
3 Tbsp. milk
5 Tbsp. ketchup, divided
2 Tbsp. Dijon mustard
½ tsp. salt
¼ tsp. black pepper
1 lb. 85% lean ground beef
2 Tbsp. mayonnaise
1 loaf soft French bread (5 to 6 inches wide)
3 Tbsp. butter, softened
4 oz. Muenster cheese, sliced
¾ cup arugula

1. Preheat oven to 350°F. In a large bowl combine bread crumbs, egg, onion, pickle, milk, 2 tablespoons ketchup, 1 tablespoon mustard, salt, and pepper. Add beef; mix well. Shape into a 4×5-inch loaf and place in a 2-quart baking dish. Bake 1 hour and 10 minutes or until done (165°F). Remove from oven; let stand 5 minutes. Turn oven to broil.

2. Meanwhile, for sauce, stir together remaining 3 tablespoons ketchup, 1 tablespoon mustard, and the mayonnaise. Cover and chill.

3. Cut bread into eight ¾-inch slices. (You may not use entire loaf.) Lightly butter both sides of bread and place on one end of a large baking sheet. Broil 4 to 5 inches from the heat source 1 to 2 minutes or until lightly toasted; turn slices. Slice meat loaf into four 5-inch long slices. Place on other end of baking sheet and top with cheese. Broil 1 to 2 minutes more or until bread is lightly toasted and cheese is melted. Assemble sandwiches using toasted bread, meat loaf, arugula, and sauce. Makes 4 servings.

PER SERVING 749 cal., 43 g fat (19 g sat. fat), 178 mg chol., 1,582 mg sodium, 51 g carb., 2 g fiber, 9 g sugars, 39 g pro.

RAVIOLI LASAGNA WITH BABY KALE AND ITALIAN SAUSAGE

RAVIOLI LASAGNA WITH BABY KALE AND ITALIAN SAUSAGE

PREP 25 minutes
BAKE 55 minutes at 375°F

1 5- to 6-oz. pkg. baby kale, coarsely chopped
12 oz. Italian-flavor cooked chicken sausage, chopped
1½ cups shredded mozzarella cheese (6 oz.)
½ cup snipped fresh basil
1 28-oz. can no-salt-added crushed tomatoes
1 14.5-oz. can fire-roasted diced tomatoes with garlic, undrained
1 8-oz. can no-salt-added tomato sauce
1 tsp. dried Italian seasoning, crushed
½ tsp. fennel seeds, crushed
2 9-oz. pkg. refrigerated cheese-filled ravioli

Grated Parmesan cheese (optional)

1. Preheat oven to 375°F. Grease a 9×13-inch baking pan. In a bowl combine kale, sausage, ¾ cup of the mozzarella cheese, and the basil. For sauce, in another bowl combine the next five ingredients (through fennel seeds).

2. Spread about 1 cup of the sauce in the prepared dish. Top with one package ravioli and half the kale mixture. Spoon another 1 cup sauce over kale mixture. Top with remaining ravioli and kale mixture. Spoon over remaining sauce. Sprinkle with remaining ¾ cup mozzarella.

3. Cover with nonstick or greased foil. Bake 30 minutes. Remove foil; bake 25 minutes more or until heated. If desired, top with Parmesan cheese and additional basil. Makes 8 servings.

PER SERVING 378 cal., 13 g fat (7 g sat. fat), 82 mg chol., 858 mg sodium, 40 g carb., 6 g fiber, 10 g sugars, 24 g pro.

CHOCOLATE CHUNK AND CARAMEL PECAN PIE

PREP 35 minutes
COOK 30 minutes
COOL 30 minutes
BAKE 45 minutes at 350°F

½   cup butter
¾   cup light-color corn syrup
⅔   cup granulated sugar
⅔   cup packed brown sugar
2   Tbsp. bourbon or water
½   tsp. fleur de sel or other fine sea salt
1   cup heavy cream
2   tsp. vanilla
    Pastry for Single-Crust Pie (recipe page 95)
3   eggs, lightly beaten
2½ cups pecan halves
6   oz. dark, bittersweet, or semisweet chocolate, chopped

1. For caramel sauce, in a medium saucepan heat butter over low heat until melted, stirring frequently. Stir in corn syrup, granulated sugar, brown sugar, the bourbon, and ½ teaspoon fleur de sel. Bring to boiling over medium heat, stirring constantly; reduce heat. Boil gently, uncovered, about 30 minutes or until reduced to 1¾ cups, stirring frequently. Remove from heat. Carefully whisk in cream and vanilla. Cool 30 minutes.
2. Meanwhile, preheat oven to 350°F. Prepare Pastry for Single-Crust Pie. On a lightly floured surface, use your hands to slightly flatten dough. Roll pastry into a 12-inch circle. Transfer pastry to a 9-inch pie plate, being careful not to stretch pastry. Trim pastry to ½ inch beyond edge of plate; crimp edge as desired.
3. For filling, transfer 1¼ cups of the caramel sauce to a large bowl. Stir in eggs until combined. Stir in pecans and chocolate. Pour filling into pastry shell. Cover edge of pie with foil to prevent overbrowning. Bake 25 minutes. Remove foil. Bake 20 minutes more or until filling is set. Cool on a wire rack.
4. To serve, reheat the remaining caramel sauce over low heat. Spoon some of the warm sauce over pie. Sprinkle lightly with additional fleur de sel. If desired, serve with remaining sauce. Makes 10 servings.
PER SERVING *788 cal., 54 g fat (21 g sat. fat), 126 mg chol., 443 mg sodium, 76 g carb., 4 g fiber, 56 g sugars, 8 g pro.*

STREUSEL BERRY BARS

PREP 20 minutes
BAKE 50 minutes at 350°F
COOL 2 hours

    Nonstick cooking spray
1½ cups butter, softened
2   cups granulated sugar
2   eggs
4   cups all-purpose flour
1½ cups pecans, coarsely chopped
2   10-oz. jars strawberry preserves or seedless red raspberry preserves
1   recipe Powdered Sugar Icing or sifted powdered sugar

1. Preheat oven to 350°F. Line a 9×13-inch baking pan with foil, extending foil over edges of pan;. Lightly coat foil with cooking spray. Set pan aside.
2. In a large bowl beat butter and granulated sugar with a mixer on medium until combined, scraping bowl as needed. Beat in eggs. Beat in as much flour as you can with the mixer. Stir in any remaining flour and the pecans (mixture will be crumbly). Remove 2 cups of the pecan mixture for topping.
3. Press the remaining pecan mixture into the bottom of the prepared baking pan. Bake 15 minutes. Carefully spread preserves to within ½ inch of edges. Sprinkle reserved topping over preserves.
4. Bake 35 minutes or until top is golden brown. Cool in pan on a wire rack. Drizzle with Powdered Sugar Icing. Use edges of foil to lift uncut bars out of pan. Transfer to a cutting board. Cut into bars. Makes 48 servings.
Powdered Sugar Icing In a small bowl combine 1 cup powdered sugar, 1 tablespoon milk, and ¼ teaspoon vanilla. Stir in additional milk, 1 tablespoon at a time, until icing is drizzling consistency.
PER SERVING *189 cal., 9 g fat (4 g sat. fat), 23 mg chol., 58 mg sodium, 27 g carb., 1 g fiber, 16 g sugars, 2 g pro.*

CHOCOLATE CHUNK AND CARAMEL PECAN PIE

STREUSEL
BERRY BARS

Index